THE DECADES OF TWENTIETH-CENTURY AMERICA

AMERICA IN THE 1900s

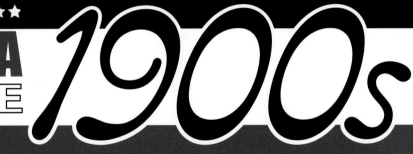

MARLENE TARG BRILL

 Twenty-First Century Books · Minneapolis

To Rich and Alison, my inspirations

Twenty-First Century Books
A division of Lerner Publishing Group, Inc.
241 First Avenue North
Minneapolis, MN 55401 U.S.A.

Website address: www.lernerbooks.com

Library of Congress Cataloging-in-Publication Data

Brill, Marlene Targ.
    America in the 1900s / by Marlene Targ Brill.
        p.   cm. — (The decades of twentieth-century America)
    Includes bibliographical references and index.
    ISBN 978–0–8225–3436–5 (lib. bdg. : alk. paper)
    1. United States—History—1901–1909—Juvenile literature. 2. United States—Social conditions—1865–1918—Juvenile literature. 3. United States—Intellectual life—1865–1918—Juvenile literature. 4. Nineteen hundreds (Decade)—Juvenile literature. I. Title.
    E756.B769 2010
    973.9—dc22   2007040983

Manufactured in the United States of America
1 2 3 4 5 6 – PA – 15 14 13 12 11 10

Contents

★★★★★★★★★★★★★★★★★★★

Crowds gather under strings of electric lights at
New York's City Hall on NEW YEAR'S EVE, 1899.

TOWARD A NEW CENTURY

*A*mericans entered the twentieth century filled with hope and confidence. The previous decade had set the nation on a course of widespread prosperity, change, and invention that made any problem seem solvable. Development spread from Atlantic to Pacific shores. A web of new railroad lines had opened the West to expansion at a rapid rate. Cities replaced unspoiled prairies and forests. Plentiful natural resources made the United States the envy of the world. By 1900 the United States had become a major industrial and political power on the global stage. American citizens believed that although many problems still existed, the future was limitless.

The United States had achieved world-class status as a result of the Spanish-American War (1898). In that conflict, U.S. president William McKinley sent the battleship USS *Maine* to neighboring Cuba in response to an uprising on the island nation. A group of Cuban rebels had revolted against Spain, which controlled Cuba at the time. McKinley sent the ship to protect U.S. citizens living in Cuba in case the unrest led to war. But when the USS *Maine* docked in Cuba's Havana Harbor, an explosion rocked its decks, killing most officers and crew. Early reports blamed Spain, although Spanish authorities claimed that their country had nothing to do with the explosion. Modern-day historians believe the explosion was an accident.

5

Nevertheless, newspapers back home stirred Americans to call for war. "Remember the *Maine*!" became a common battle cry. In anticipation of war, Assistant Secretary of the Navy Theodore Roosevelt sent a U.S. fleet to the Philippines and to other Spanish-governed regions in Pacific and Caribbean waters.

■ A MILITARY POWERHOUSE

Once President McKinley declared war on Spain, fighting lasted little more than three months before the United States triumphed. For the first time in the nation's history, the United States emerged as a military powerhouse. It took over several Spanish territories, including Cuba, the Philippines, Guam, and Puerto Rico. Equally important, the United States realized a new vision of itself. Americans had tasted the delights of expansion and empire building, and they wanted more.

Not all Americans were thrilled about expanding beyond U.S. borders. A small group of U.S. politicians—led by one-time presidential candidate William Jennings Bryan and former president Grover Cleveland—opposed expansion, setting off battles that dragged on for years. They formed the Anti-Imperialist League—a group that was against imperialism (stronger nations controlling

NEW YORK CITY IN 1900 was a city of tall buildings and busy streets. The 1900s saw the opening of new bridges and the beginning of construction of the city's subway system.

weaker nations). The League believed the Philippines and Cuba should govern themselves. Cuba did gain its freedom, but imperialist American lawmakers refused to grant self-government to the Philippines. South Dakota senator Richard Pettigrew famously argued that "bananas [a Philippine crop] and self-government do not grow on the same patch of ground."

■ EXPLODING ECONOMY

Economic growth in the 1890s had exceeded most Americans' wildest imaginations. Early in the decade, the 1893 financial panic had sent the nation into economic depression. But business leaders agreed that the economy had fully recovered by the mid-1890s. In 1900 the economy was experiencing a period of rapid growth. American businesses sold goods to newly opened markets in China and throughout other parts of Asia. Many Americans believed that bursts of sales at home and abroad were sure to enrich their nation well into the next century. William King, president of the New York Merchants' Association, wrote, "The producer from the soil has had unusual prosperity, as have the workers in mines, mills, and workshops. The tendency of all lines of manufactured goods is upward."

Exploding businesses created millionaires. But the gap between rich and poor also widened.

American farmers sold record bushels of wheat and cotton at high prices. Iron and steel exports doubled in the period from 1886 to 1895 alone and continued growing until 1900. Factories blanketed major cities, attracting workers from farms and small towns. Manufacturers believed they improved the lives of American workers by providing more hours of paid work to fill the days.

Exploding businesses created millionaires. But the gap between rich and poor also widened. Entering the new century, supercorporations emerged. These were giant companies formed to reduce or eliminate business competition. To dominate a particular industry, large corporations either bought out smaller companies or linked their businesses through mergers known as trusts or monopolies. In 1900, 185 corporate combinations ran one-third of all U.S. manufacturing investments.

Many social reformers believed that merging businesses put everyday workers at risk. They knew that corporations paid workers extremely low wages in order to increase profits for investors. Poorly paid employees lived and worked in run-down, filthy, unhealthful conditions. In the 1800s, employees had increasingly begun organizing into unions (groups that support workers' rights) to fight for better working conditions. Settlement houses in New York and Chicago began to offer social services to the poor and to new immigrants. Going into the 1900s, however, government and corporations did little to relieve the suffering of workers.

■ A NATION OF IMMIGRANTS

Between 1860 and 1900, the U.S. population skyrocketed. The number of immigrants coming through Ellis Island, New York—the main entryway into the United States—more than tripled during that time. After passing through Ellis Island, many immigrants stayed in New York City. A sizable group fanned out to expanding regions of the forty-five states that made up the union at that time.

Major U.S. cities, such as Chicago, Boston, and Philadelphia, doubled their populations as a result of immigration. Improved transportation and communication transformed cities, allowing them to spread out beyond the urban center. People with money

IMMIGRANTS ARRIVE AT ELLIS ISLAND in New York in the early 1900s. Opened in 1892, Ellis Island received up to one million new immigrants per day.

moved to the outer edges of cities, leaving poor families in the unsanitary, polluted industrial areas of the urban core.

Soaring numbers of immigrants changed the face of the United States. Earlier immigrants had come from northern and western Europe. Many were Irish and German and practiced Catholicism. Other immigrants were Protestants from Scandinavian countries. Around 1880, immigrants from southern and eastern Europe began to arrive. Coming from Poland, Russia, and Italy, they settled mostly in larger cities of the eastern United States. The newcomers followed Roman Catholic, Eastern Orthodox, and Jewish faiths, and they brought their traditions and cultural practices with them.

Even with growing industrialization, the United States in 1900 was made up mostly of rural areas and small towns. Sixty percent of the U.S. population of 76 million people lived in or around towns with fewer than twenty-five hundred inhabitants. Most families still farmed.

Ninety percent of African Americans lived in the rural South. They began migrating to northern cities to look for jobs in the first twenty years of the twentieth century. The three largest cities absorbing the greatest numbers of African Americans and immigrants were New York, Chicago, and Philadelphia. By this time, the U.S. government had forced most Native Americans in the East off their historic homelands to live on reservations in Oklahoma and Nevada.

With so many different groups converging in American cities, established centers of power (run largely by white males) felt threatened. A clash of wills had always existed between the haves and have-nots. The conflict broke out in earnest. The new decade—and century—was off with a bang.

WILLIAM MCKINLEY TAKES THE PRESIDENTIAL OATH OF OFFICE
at his inauguration ceremony in 1901

Chapter One

THEODORE ROOSEVELT'S
BIG STICK:
Politics in the 1900s

*I*n 1900 President William McKinley easily defeated William Jennings Bryan to retain his title as the twenty-fifth president of the United States. McKinley was reelected with huge public support. People loved his good character, quick mind, and warm personality.

This was the second time Bryan had run against McKinley on a platform rejecting interference in the politics of other countries. But given the recent U.S. victory in the Spanish-American War (1898) and the strong economy, voters believed the nation was on the right course with their likable president and his Republican Party. The victory at war proved so positive a mandate that McKinley selected Theodore Roosevelt, the popular war hero and sitting New York governor, as his vice president.

Just when the nation's enthusiasm for the new administration seemed strongest, disaster struck. Six months into his second term, McKinley stood in a receiving line after giving a speech at the Pan-American Exhibition in Buffalo, New York. Leon Czolgosz, a twenty-eight-year-old factory worker and anarchist (person who wants to overthrow the government) from Cleveland, Ohio, waited patiently for his turn to meet McKinley. As the line moved, the smiling president reached toward Czolgosz for a handshake. Czolgosz whipped a handkerchief off his pistol-carrying hand and shot McKinley in the stomach.

11

The wounded president clung to life for eight days before dying on September 14, 1901. Nine days later, Czolgosz went to trial. A confession he had made to police after they arrested him was admitted as evidence in the trial. In that confession, Czolgosz had suggested that he killed the president because he didn't think one person should have so much power.

After a two-day trial, the jury weighed the evidence for just thirty minutes. They found Czolgosz guilty of murder, and on September 27, Czolgosz was put to death in the electric chair.

■ THE VICE PRESIDENT TAKES OVER

The country was heartbroken by the president's assassination. Vice President Theodore Roosevelt did his best to console an uneasy nation. At his swearing in, he said in a broken voice, "In this hour of deep and terrible national bereavement, I wish to state that it shall be my aim to continue absolutely unbroken the policy of President McKinley for the peace, prosperity and honor of our beloved country."

Although he agreed with some of McKinley's plans, Roosevelt had definite ideas about the country's direction on a domestic level and about its involvement in the affairs of other countries. This worried several lawmakers. Few doubted Roosevelt's bravery. He had taken a ragtag group of fighters called the Rough Riders to Cuba during the Spanish-American War and led them to defeat Spanish soldiers in the Battle of San Juan. But many saw Roosevelt as a brash cowboy who bullied his way into leadership positions. To carry his troops to Cuba, he had hijacked a U.S. military ship. Roosevelt seemed such a loose cannon that New York senator Mark

THEODORE ROOSEVELT AROUND 1903. Two years earlier, at age forty-two, he had become the youngest person to hold the office of president.

Hanna had expressed unease with his appointment as vice president. "Don't you realize that there's only one life between that madman and the Presidency?" Hanna had warned.

Roosevelt assumed the presidency with the same zest and determination he mustered for everything he did. As a sickly youngster, he had lifted weights and exercised until his body matched his probing mind in strength. At forty-two, he was the United States' youngest president and a commanding personality. By nature, his energy and keen political eye far exceeded those of most politicians of any age. Since he had not been elected, he came to the office unburdened with the baggage of owing political favors. And Roosevelt cared little what others thought. He moved quickly to launch programs that put his own stamp on the new administration.

■ DIGGING THE PANAMA CANAL

Roosevelt believed that the economic and political influence of the United States should extend overseas. He saw this expansion as helpful for those nations he viewed as less developed. He thought such nations needed guidance from a bigger, more established country. To boost U.S. presence abroad, Roosevelt expanded and modernized the U.S. Navy. To cement U.S. sea power, he also wanted to build a canal across Central America as a passageway between the Atlantic and Pacific oceans. Until this time, ships moving between the two oceans had to sail all the way around South America. A Central American canal would dramatically reduce travel time between the oceans. With the canal, naval ships could more easily monitor and protect the seas throughout the growing U.S. empire.

The idea for a canal was not new. A French engineering company had begun digging a canal through the Isthmus of Panama in 1882. (An isthmus is a narrow piece of land between two bodies of water.) But the project had stalled due to construction problems and to deaths from tropical diseases.

At the time, the South American nation of Colombia controlled Panama, and France held rights to the canal. Roosevelt wasted no time in securing Panama and seeking rights to the canal so the United States could begin construction.

In 1903 Roosevelt asked Secretary of State John Hay to negotiate with Colombia to create a treaty that would

Steam shovels cut the deep trench that would eventually become the **PANAMA CANAL**.

give the United States the right to build the canal. But Colombia rejected the treaty. Roosevelt called the Colombian government a bunch of "irresponsible bandits." Behind the scenes, he lent support to a revolt in Panama, where rebels wanted to break away from Colombia and make their own treaty with the United States. Panama won its independence, and Roosevelt offered the rebels ten million dollars for rights to the canal. After the rebels accepted, Roosevelt sent U.S. Marines to support a team of engineers. In 1904 the U.S. Congress approved the contract with a long-term lease. Contractors began digging in the 10-mile (16-kilometer) canal zone.

Roosevelt was a hands-on leader who supervised everything his administration touched. He monitored the Panama Canal by traveling to the construction site, tramping through the mud, and testing equipment. This historic trip confirmed Roosevelt as the first president to visit another country while in office.

Although it took another ten years to complete, the Panama Canal became Roosevelt's crowning foreign policy achievement. The project also brought great fame to its supervisor and future U.S. president, William Howard Taft. The completed canal saved ships weeks in travel time by cutting out about 7,872 miles (12,668 km) from the trip between New York on the East Coast and San Francisco on the West Coast. Roosevelt liked to say the canal represented his approach to foreign policy, which he often summed up with the phrase, "Speak softly, and carry a big stick."

Ohio native William Howard Taft was smart, kind, and driven to succeed. He quickly rose through the ranks of the legal profession to various high-ranking judgeships. On his climb to the nation's top courts, he caught the attention of lawmakers. President McKinley chose him to serve as governor of the Philippines, a position he held from 1901 to 1904. Under Taft's supervision, Filipinos built dams, schools, and sewage systems. Taft established the island nation's first independent legal system and distributed land once owned by the Roman Catholic Church to local peasants.

Taft's leadership ability was tested as U.S. secretary of war from 1904 to 1908. Working under Roosevelt, Taft had managed the Panama Canal construction and restored order in Cuba after its 1906 civil war. At home he organized emergency care after an extremely destructive earthquake hit San Francisco that same year.

In 1908 Roosevelt supported Taft as the Republican Party's candidate for president. Roosevelt had decided not to run for the office again and thought Taft perfect to continue his progressive policies. But newspaper reporters constantly compared the two presidents, with Taft often coming off poorly. Roosevelt was a tough outdoorsman, while Taft became the first president to take up the slow-paced sport of golf while in office. While Roosevelt seemed to be in constant motion, Taft nodded off frequently, sometimes during meetings with senators. He fell asleep so many times

WILLIAM HOWARD TAFT (1857–1930) achieved a lifelong dream when he became chief justice of the United States in 1921.

during automobile rides with his wife that she nicknamed him Sleeping Beauty.

Once friends, Roosevelt and Taft eventually parted ways over Taft's handling of environmental and business issues. By the 1912 presidential election, Roosevelt was calling his former friend a fathead. Roosevelt decided to challenge Taft for office that year. He ran as a Progressive, while Taft ran as a Republican. But both men lost to Democratic candidate Woodrow Wilson, who became the United States' twenty-eighth president.

Eight years after leaving the White House, President Warren G. Harding nominated Taft to the U.S. Supreme Court in 1921. With this appointment, Taft became the only president to serve as both president and chief justice. Taft held another distinction as well. He began the custom of U.S. presidents opening the professional baseball season by throwing the first pitch

■ ROOSEVELT AS MEDIATOR

During his years in office, Roosevelt employed military force cautiously but was unafraid to send troops and weapons to protect U.S. interests. He used a combination of military might and diplomacy to resolve differences between countries. For example, in 1902 Roosevelt appealed to the International Court of Arbitration in The Hague, Netherlands, to resolve disagreements between the United States and Mexico. (The two nations could not agree on which country was responsible for supporting Roman Catholic missions, or religious communities, in California—which had once been part of Mexico.) The International Court of Arbitration had been established as a means to settle conflicts between nations peacefully. Since the court's founding in 1899, however, no country had asked for its help. Roosevelt's gesture reduced tensions between the United States and Mexico and thus encouraged other nations to choose negotiation over fighting.

While Roosevelt addressed concerns in Latin America, unrest was building in the Far East. Russia had occupied Manchuria (modern northern China) in 1900 to suppress rebels there and was refusing to leave. In fact, Russian troops expanded eastward into Korea. This move particularly troubled nearby Japan. The Japanese responded by firing on Russia's invading naval fleet in Lushun, a port in northeastern China. Immediately afterward, Japan sank all Russian battleships in the area and declared war against Russia. President Roosevelt asserted the United States' neutrality in the conflict.

As the Russo-Japanese War (1904–1905) came to a close, President Roosevelt offered a site in Portsmouth, New Hampshire, where the two countries could negotiate a peace treaty. At the meetings, he assisted with negotiations. The talks proved successful, and Roosevelt took much of the credit. His work earned him a Nobel Peace Prize in 1906. Roosevelt was the first American to win a Nobel Prize in any category. Gunnar Knudsen from the Nobel Committee told U.S. ambassador Herbert H. D. Pierce at the award presentation:

> The United States of America was among the first to infuse the ideal of peace into practical politics. . . . But what has especially directed the attention of the friends of peace and of the whole civilized world to

Russian and Japanese delegates negotiate **THE TREATY OF PORTSMOUTH** in New Hampshire in 1905. President Roosevelt's role in arranging the peace talks between the two countries earned him the Nobel Peace Price in 1906.

the United States is President Roosevelt's happy role in bringing to an end the bloody war recently waged between two of the world's great powers, Japan and Russia.

■ THE PRESIDENT SHOWS MORE MUSCLE

The peace prize did not interfere with Roosevelt's willingness to use forceful methods when he thought it necessary. In 1907, for example, hostilities increased between the United States and Japan. Japan feared the growing U.S. influence in China. To ease tensions with Japan, Roosevelt ordered a series of public and private meetings. But he also sent a fleet to Japan to impress its government with U.S. naval strength. The show of force encouraged Japan to enter negotiations, which eased the tension between the two countries.

The emerging agreement between the United States and Japan influenced how the United States treated Japanese immigrants. Until 1905 Japanese workers and their families had suffered severe discrimination in the United

> ## " Speak softly, and carry a big stick. "

—Theodore Roosevelt describing his approach to foreign policy, 1903

States. For instance, schools in San Francisco, California, segregated Japanese schoolchildren rather than allow them in classes with other children. Roosevelt's "Gentleman's Agreement" with Japanese officials resulted in the California school board agreeing to end segregation of Japanese students if Japan would agree to limit the number of Japanese workers coming to the United States.

In another major foreign policy move, Roosevelt expanded the Monroe Doctrine of 1823. The Monroe Doctrine said that European nations would stay out of the affairs in the Western Hemisphere. Roosevelt was convinced that Germany might interfere with affairs in Venezuela, and he used the Monroe Doctrine to keep Germany away.

■ THE 1904 ELECTION

In 1904 Roosevelt ran for president against Democrat Alton Parker. By this time, Roosevelt was the leader of the growing progressive movement—a reform crusade to protect ordinary citizens from government waste and corruption. Roosevelt called his campaign the Square Deal because he believed every American should receive a square (fair) deal from their government. He pledged to end unjust business practices, enact stricter corporate regulations, and conserve the nation's natural resources. These were promises people understood, and they were drawn to Roosevelt's enthusiasm and charms. In 1904 he was elected to his first full term as president by the largest majority of any candidate to date.

"Victory. Triumph. My Father is elected. . . . An unprecedented landslide," wrote Roosevelt's daughter Alice in her diary on November 8, 1904.

ith Theodore Roosevelt as commander in chief, adventure and expansion were goals that the United States valued. And nothing captures the spirit of expansion like the exploration of exotic lands. U.S. explorer Robert Peary and his aide, African American civil engineer Matthew Henson, went on some of the greatest journeys of exploration of the early 1900s. They undertook a twelve-year quest to reach the icy North Pole. President Roosevelt, himself a robust explorer, encouraged men like Peary. Roosevelt admired their ruggedness and patriotism. Other less hardy individuals funded these explorations to win glory for themselves and the institutions they represented.

For example, several of Peary's expeditions were funded by the American Museum of Natural History in New York. The museum had supported Peary's exploration of Greenland in 1896 and hoped he would head north again to reach the North Pole in the early 1900s.

On March 1, 1909, Peary and Henson led a crew of twenty-three men, 133 dogs, and nineteen sleds from Canada's Ellesmere Island. For the next month, the explorers battled −50°F (−46°C) temperatures and snow-covered, frozen land. Temperatures plunged so low that Peary's parka cracked like glass, and the brandy in his flask froze

ROBERT PEARY wore warm fur garments like the Inuit people he met in the Arctic. In this picture from the early 1900s, he stands in one of the boats used for exploration.

solid. By April 6, only six explorers remained. But Peary, Henson, and four Inuit men managed that day to pierce the barren North Pole snow with the U. S. flag. Once he had achieved his goal, Peary returned south to Canada. He wrote in his diary about his accomplishment: "The Pole at last. The prize of three centuries. My dream and goal for twenty years. Mine at last!"

Southwestern Oregon's CRATER LAKE has some of the purest water in the United States. As president, Theodore Roosevelt took action in 1902 to protect the lake and the forests that surround it.

Chapter Two

POLITICS OF THE LAND:

Protecting Natural Resources

By the 1900s, the continental United States had been explored end to end and settlements dotted even the most remote areas. With this growth came regional differences. The East, with its crowded cities and old-line families, was home to the financial power brokers and corporate deal makers. The Midwest included a mix of open farmland and urban industrial centers. Midwestern transportation hubs, such as Chicago, Illinois, and Saint Louis, Missouri, surpassed many eastern cities in population and manufacturing inventiveness. The West, although more sparsely populated, supplied eastern businesses with a steady stream of natural resources that came from mining and cow towns in the Dakotas, California, and Washington State. Montana alone produced 23 percent of the world's copper supply. And oil gushers, or "black gold," had just been discovered in Beaumont, Texas.

■ ROOSEVELT'S LOVE OF NATURE

Roosevelt was the first president to champion progressive causes that took all regions of the country into account. As a nature lover, he placed a priority on the impact government policies and the economy had on the nation's natural treasures. Roosevelt had always loved science and the outdoors. He rode horses, hunted wild animals, and climbed mountains. He also devoured books about nature. His fondness for the outdoors and the creatures who lived there seemed limitless.

One famed story told of a trip Roosevelt took while president to resolve a border conflict between Mississippi and Louisiana. During his free time on that trip, Roosevelt went bear hunting. He was unable to kill a bear, so his assistants roped one for him to shoot. President Roosevelt flatly refused. How could he shoot a defenseless bear?

Reporters found the bear story endearing. Political cartoonist Clifford Berryman drew a cartoon showing the mustached president in his usual cowboy hat refusing to shoot a scared, roped bear cub. The cartoon, "Drawing the Line in Mississippi," appeared in newspapers around the country. The title reflected both the border dispute and the president's consideration for the bear. The cartoon caught the attention of Rose and Morris Michtom, a Brooklyn, New York, couple who owned a candy shop. The Michtoms wrote the president for permission to call a stuffed toy that Rose was sewing a "teddy bear." After Roosevelt agreed, the Michtoms displayed the bear in their store window. Teddy bears became an instant hit, allowing the Michtoms to expand their small business and become the Ideal Novelty and Toy Company.

U.S. wilderness explorer John Muir believed that if Roosevelt was that

---

CLIFFORD BERRYMAN DREW "DRAWING THE LINE IN MISSISSIPPI" for the *Washington Post* in 1902. It shows Roosevelt refusing to shoot a helpless bear cub while on a hunting trip near the border of Mississippi and Louisiana.

PRESIDENT ROOSEVELT'S TRAVEL PARTY stopped here at Yosemite's Inspiration Point in California on the way to nearby Glacier Point during a 1903 tour.

committed to land and animals, he should battle those who opposed preserving the environment. Muir had recently founded the Sierra Club to organize individuals who supported the idea of creating protected national parks to benefit all citizens. One day in 1903, Muir invited Roosevelt to leave his Secret Service men behind and camp with him in California near awe-inspiring Glacier Point, in what eventually became Yosemite National Park. Legend says that Roosevelt found the site so breathtaking, he committed himself to preserving nature on the spot. Roosevelt transformed his lifelong love of nature into public policies that aimed to conserve the land and its resources.

■ CONSERVATION LAWS

In the early 1900s, debates flared throughout the nation about the use of land and resources. Expansionists believed the land and resources should be available for the taking as long as they lasted. Conservationists preferred to preserve the country's storehouse of natural wealth and beauty.

JOHN MUIR was the first person to suggest that the movement of glaciers (huge sheets of ice) formed Arizona's Grand Canyon.

John Muir was an author, artist, explorer, scientist, and inventor. But he was most acclaimed for his love of nature. That devotion led him to wage lifelong battles to establish and preserve U.S. national parks. The Sierra Club, which he founded in 1892, called him the Father of Our National Park System.

Muir was born in Scotland in 1838 and raised on a farm near Portage, Wisconsin. His demanding father required him to labor from sunup to sundown. Still, young Muir found time to roam the lush fields and woods of Wisconsin. Self-taught, Muir read every night and figured math problems from wood chips he chopped. He carved pieces of wood into practical inventions, such as safety locks, clocks, and devices for feeding horses.

Muir attended the University of Wisconsin but left college to travel the northern United States and Canada. He supported himself with odd jobs. Muir eventually took a job in an Indianapolis, Indiana, carriage shop. Here he suffered an accident that temporarily blinded him. Muir's hand slipped when he was working with a file, and the tip of the file jabbed his right eye. The vision in his left eye failed too due to the extra stress. The accident changed his life and cemented his commitment to nature. About his accident, he explained in 1867: "I felt neither pain nor faintness, the thought was so tremendous . . . that I should never look at a flower again."

When his vision returned, Muir decided to dedicate his life to exploring nature. He journeyed through much of the United States, traveling on foot to stay close to the land. On one occasion, Muir discovered an Alaskan glacier that was later named Muir Glacier in his honor. But he always returned to California's Sierra Nevada, the mountain range he loved best.

Muir's travels eventually took him to other countries and continents. He explored Australia, South America, China, Japan, and parts of Europe and Africa. Muir compared glaciers in other countries with those in Yosemite National Park and developed new theories about how glaciers form. He wrote magazine articles and books on his findings.

Muir established the Sierra Club for people who wanted to "do something for wildness and make the mountains glad." In 1901 Muir wrote *Our National Parks,* a book about U.S. forests. This book attracted Roosevelt's attention and led Muir to invite the president to Glacier Point in Yosemite. They viewed the majestic rocks and glistening waterfalls that inspired Roosevelt's conservation policy. Muir's conservation work lasted until his death in 1914. By then he had published more than six books and 150 articles and earned many honors.

President Roosevelt, with his love of the outdoors, lent his weight to the conservationists. He was the first president to do so.

By the time Roosevelt entered office, much of the nation's forested land had been logged or turned into farms. Less than 20 percent of the country's original forests remained. Overuse of farmland in the South and East had depleted the soil. Unregulated use of water (the practice of allowing individuals to use as much water as they like) threatened neighboring regions with floods and drought. And aggressive oil, gas, and mineral industries freely mined resources without concern for the changes mining created in the landscape. They didn't worry about what might happen to the land, animals, and people left behind once the companies had moved on. Muir and Sierra Club members swayed the president toward a long-term view of the land and natural resources.

Loggers survey **A CLEARED SECTION OF FOREST IN THE CASCADE MOUNTAINS** near Seattle, Washington, around 1906.

"The time has fully arrived for recognizing in the law the responsibility to the community, the state, and the nation which rests upon the private owners of private lands," Roosevelt said of his decision to embrace conservation laws. "The ownership of land is a public trust. The man who would so handle his forest as to cause erosion and to injure stream flow must be not only educated but he must be controlled."

Roosevelt's earliest conservation move was to work with Congress to pass the Newlands Reclamation Act of 1902, named for Representative Francis Newlands of Nevada. This new law authorized federal construction of water projects—such as reservoirs and dams—in the western United States. The water projects would be funded by the sale of public land. Over the next few years, many aspects of the water projects proved difficult to administer. But as a result of the law, the U.S. government hired workers to build very large dams, which harnessed water as a way to control flooding; to water crops; and eventually to provide electrical power.

Other conservation actions followed. Under the Transfer Act of 1905, Roosevelt created the U.S. Forest Service to oversee the nation's forest reserves. The head of the agency, conservationist Gifford Pinchot, brought scientific and management skills to preserve western timberlands. His goal and Roosevelt's was to

Tourists visit the famous **PETRIFIED BRIDGE IN ARIZONA'S PETRIFIED FOREST** around 1908. President Roosevelt ordered that the area be protected for scientific study.

"The ownership of land is a public trust."

—*Theodore Roosevelt speaking to Congress, 1909*

balance businesses' interest in the land with that of preservationists. Pinchot created a policy of selective cutting, which allowed lumber companies to thin out a forest's trees without wiping out the forest.

In 1906 the American Antiquities Act safeguarded huge tracts of land, such as the Grand Canyon in Arizona and Devils Tower in Wyoming. The next year, the Inland Waterways Commission was created to govern what happened to the nation's rivers and streams. For the rest of the decade, Roosevelt wrestled with state governments to set aside large areas of land for public use. These tracts became the country's first system of national parks, forests, and bird sanctuaries. Roosevelt's prodding preserved such national treasures as Crater Lake National Park in Oregon, Wind Cave National Park in South Dakota (which became a game preserve in 1912), and Arizona's Petrified Forest—one of the world's largest and most colorful clusters of fossilized wood. Roosevelt canceled the sale of almost 80 million acres (32 million hectares) of mineral-rich land to mining companies and gained another 1.5 million acres (607,000 hectares) for future water-related projects. He pried millions of acres of forest from lumber industries. By the end of his term, Roosevelt was credited with saving more than 170 million acres (69 million hectares) of land for national parks and monuments.

27

On April 18, 1906, the ground rumbled along 296 miles (477 km) of California's San Andreas Fault (a series of cracks in Earth's surface), from northwest of San Juan Bautista to Cape Mendocino—California's westernmost point. San Franciscans felt the first shock at 5:12 A.M. Twenty seconds later, the ground seemed to explode. People even felt the shaking in Oregon and Nevada.

The earthquake lasted less than one minute, but it produced the nation's most devastating natural disaster in history. It caused buildings to collapse, sending hailstorms of bricks and mortar onto streets and sidewalks. Many people lay crushed under piles of broken wood and debris. Streetcar tracks sat twisted and mangled, and downed electrical wires hung uncertainly in all directions. Shock waves broke water mains, destroying the city's water supply.

The worst threat came from fierce fires ignited by the earthquake. At first, firefighters pumped water from the nearby San Francisco Bay to save businesses and office buildings. But as the fire pushed inward, fire trucks were unable to calm the

Women search through the rubble of their home after the SAN FRANCISCO EARTHQUAKE.

blazes without the city's regular supply of water. To stop the furious flames from spreading, police dynamited buildings that might provide fuel to the fires. They shot to death helpless people caught under debris rather than let them die horribly, consumed by advancing flames.

Fires raged for three days before finally dying out. Afterward, city leaders estimated the destruction. Approximately twenty-five hundred people had died, and many more were left homeless. Almost five hundred city blocks and twenty-five thousand buildings had been ruined. Final estimates of the damage totaled around $350 million.

■ ROOSEVELT'S OTHER DOMESTIC ACHIEVEMENTS

Popular writers admired Roosevelt's spirit of reform. Journalists and authors built public support for reform by writing about the country's ills. Roosevelt generally approved of these writers' social criticisms. But when the critics began exposing widespread scandals in politics, he believed they had gone too far. He called the writers muckrakers after a character in John Bunyan's novel *Pilgrim's Progress* (1678, 1684) who was so focused on profit that he could not turn his attention to spiritual matters. Roosevelt said that muckrakers (literally, someone with a rake for handling dung and other waste material) "are often indispensable to . . . society, but only if they know when to stop raking the muck."

Yet muckrakers had a major and very positive influence on the nation's health standards. In the early 1900s, hazards involving food and medicine were largely ignored. For example, medicines mixed in pharmacies were often laced with addictive alcohol, morphine, or cocaine. Beef supplies sent to troops during the Spanish-American War contained harmful preservatives. At the time, powerful beef and pharmaceutical lobbyists—individuals hired by the livestock and drug industries to pressure Congress on their behalf—pressed lawmakers to oppose any restrictions on foods and medicines. But things changed after President Roosevelt and other reformers read Upton Sinclair's *The Jungle* in 1906. The popular novel described the filthy, stomach-churning practices involved in preparing meat products in Chicago stockyards. Public outrage and Roosevelt's

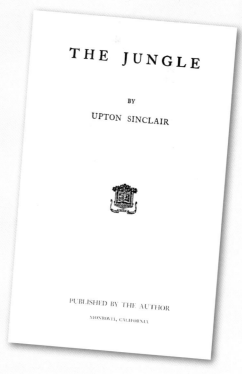

THE JUNGLE

BY

UPTON SINCLAIR

PUBLISHED BY THE AUTHOR
MONROVIA, CALIFORNIA

Upton Sinclair's **THE JUNGLE** was published in 1906.

Butchers cut up sides of pork in a **MEATPACKING HOUSE IN CHICAGO** around 1904. In his novel *The Jungle*, Upton Sinclair described unsanitary practices and terrible conditions for workers in places such as this.

backing of new laws forced sweeping changes on a national scale. In 1906 Congress finally passed the Pure Food and Drug Act. Under this law, the government created a Food and Drug Administration (FDA) to oversee testing and inspection of all foods and drugs sold for human consumption. For the first time, the government established national standards of cleanliness for slaughterhouses and food processing plants. If people got sick from food or medicine anywhere in the country, lawmakers had the legal right to conduct

Public outrage and Roosevelt's backing of new laws forced sweeping changes on a national scale.

inspections in the factories where the products were made, to determine what had gone wrong. The legislation proved a high point in progressive reform and Roosevelt's domestic agenda.

■ THE NEXT PRESIDENT

In 1908 Roosevelt announced that his two terms as president were enough. He endorsed his friend and Secretary of War William Howard Taft for president. Taft had carried out important missions for Roosevelt in the Philippines and in Panama. Roosevelt found Taft a partner in his vision to expand the United States' role overseas while conserving the environment at home.

The new president—who took office in 1909—proved a more conservative leader than Roosevelt. Taft was less willing to take great risks. He lacked the energy and flexibility to keep several warring political factions (groups) in line. His all-or-nothing way of dealing with situations eventually cost him politically and with the public.

The downward spiral of Taft's administration began after Taft fired Gifford Pinchot from his position as head of the U.S. Forest Service. Taft's secretary of the interior and Pinchot's boss, Richard Ballinger, had transferred 100,000 acres (40,468 hectares) of government-owned, coal-rich Alaskan land to investor friends. Pinchot publicly accused his boss of reassigning the land improperly. A congressional committee investigated Pinchot's accusation and cleared Ballinger of any wrongdoing. The following year, however, Ballinger resigned due to other charges of corruption. Yet Taft fired Pinchot for refusing to withdraw his accusations. When newspapers reported the story, Taft faced harsh public criticism and unfavorable comparisons to Roosevelt. One critic wrote:

> Dear Teddy, I need you; come home to me quick,
> I am worried and weary and worn.
> And as hope long deferred only makes the heart sick,
> I am sadly in need of your potent "Big Stick."

31

A woman demonstrates a sewing machine in A MODEL HOME FROM THE EARLY
1900s. The home features some of the most advanced—and most expensive—
amenities of the time, including a gas chandelier and an elegant black-leaded oven.

Chapter Three

NOVEL IDEAS FOR EVERYDAY LIVING:
Science, Technology, and Communication

*I*n the early 1900s, many of the conveniences that make modern life easier, such as electric household appliances, did not yet exist. And most lifesaving medicines and diagnostic tests had not been invented. Americans had no computers or televisions for entertainment. Even radios, refrigerators, and washing machines were about as common as the Land of Oz. With fewer labor-saving machines to do the work, most Americans had to tackle everyday chores by hand, which required great strength and endurance as well as large investments of time.

INVENTING THE ORDINARY

Many products and concepts that Americans take for granted in the twenty-first century first entered mainstream America during the early 1900s. Scores of inventors of the day devised solutions to common problems. Some creative thinkers advanced new theories or developed newfangled gadgets never before imaginable.

Thomas Edison, a self-taught electronics wizard in New Jersey, churned out new and improved inventions on a regular basis. He had invented the lightbulb in 1879, and during the 1900s, he and his scientific team developed even more improvements. These inventions made electricity more affordable, widespread in urban areas, and adaptable to new appliances.

Meanwhile, other American scientists invented amazing products. Eldridge Johnson opened the Victor Talking Machine Company in 1901 to manufacture the Victrola phonograph—an early music player for the home. The Victrola was enormously popular. Families listened from their living rooms and danced to music spun on records (large vinyl disks with grooves that allowed a needle to transmit lively tunes).

The possibilities for transmitting voices and music mechanically continued to lure inventors. In 1905 a jukebox—a machine that plays records automatically— that could play up to twenty-four songs was invented. In 1908 factories rolled out new player pianos, each with eighty-eight notes. Player pianos contained special mechanisms that allowed the instruments to play music by themselves.

A Mississippi farmer and his daughter listen to music on a **VICTROLA HOME PHONOGRAPH** around 1901.

A family takes their **KODAK BROWNIE CAMERA** on vacation. This picture appeared in an advertisement for the Brownie around 1900.

Photography also took a giant leap forward during the 1900s. The Eastman Kodak Company of New Jersey produced the first Brownie camera in 1900. Photographers paid one dollar for the Brownie black box and fifteen cents per roll of film. The 6-by-4-inch (15-by-10-centimeter) camera was small and inexpensive, and the film was fast—allowing ordinary citizens to take their own photographs rather than paying a studio photographer to take an expensive portrait. The Brownie camera replaced heavy, time-consuming, and costly equipment, which required the subject to hold a formal pose for a painfully long time.

Several new products eased the chores of daily life. For example, in 1908 James Spangler received a patent for a gadget he created by adding a fan motor and a handle to a carpet sweeper.

The device was the first portable electric vacuum cleaner. General Electric introduced the first clothes iron with a detachable cord in 1903 and the first electric toaster in 1909. In 1902 the Blickensderfer Typewriter Company produced the first electric typewriter for commercial use. About the same time, King Camp Gillette began manufacturing the double-edged safety razor with disposable blades. These razors were easy to use and didn't require sharpening, as did straight razors. Electric-powered washing machines also made their debut in the early 1900s. One of the first manufacturers of electric-powered washing machines was General Electric. The company's ad read: "If every father did the family washing next Monday, there would be an electric washing machine in every home by Saturday night."

35

Among all the early twentieth-century inventors, George Washington Carver stands out for the number and breadth of his inventions. His inspiration for invention came from his childhood on a Missouri plantation, where he was born around 1864 as the sickly son of slaves. Because he lacked enough strength for fieldwork, Carver learned about gardening instead. His skill with reviving dying plants earned him the nickname plant doctor.

Young Carver taught himself to read, as no school near his home would admit African Americans. At about the age of eleven, Carver left the plantation to find a school he could attend. He took odd jobs to earn enough to pay for shelter, going from town to town searching for better schools.

In 1890 Carver entered Simpson College in Indianola, Iowa. He transferred to Iowa State Agricultural College in Ames in 1891, where he earned a bachelor's degree in agriculture in 1894. His experiments with plants attracted so much attention that Iowa State offered him a faculty position while he studied for an advanced degree. He was the first African American to receive such an offer at the college.

Carver's fame reached Booker T. Washington, an African American educator who had helped to found the all-black Tuskegee Institute in Alabama. Washington invited Carver to direct Tuskegee's agricultural department. Carver taught and did research at Tuskegee.

In his first project, he worked to help southern farmers. At the time, much of the

GEORGE WASHINGTON CARVER displays a clump of soil in a field in Alabama.

South depended on farming. Yet much of the region's soil was no longer rich enough in nutrients to support crops, and many farmers were facing financial ruin. Carver taught farmers how to rotate crops so that the soil could replenish itself. He suggested planting peas and sweet potatoes instead of cotton. He also suggested planting peanuts. Peanuts grow in pods that feed on nitrogen in the air. The plants take in nitrogen and pass it naturally into the soil. When farmers questioned the value of peanuts, Carver determined to prove their worth.

Carver eventually developed more than three hundred uses for peanuts. He wrote books and articles to share his knowledge before he died in 1943. Carver's many honors include a monument dedicated to him in Missouri and induction into the National Inventors Hall of Fame in 1990. But he claimed that his greatest achievement was knowing his work had helped people.

The early 1900s also saw the invention of many new food and drink products. These included Hershey's Milk Chocolate Bars (1900), instant coffee (about 1901), Kellogg's Corn Flakes (1906), and tea bags (about 1908). Leo Baekeland's 1907 invention of Bakelite produced the first synthetic plastic, which led to the manufacture of affordable plastic containers and appliances.

Other inventions of the era included bottle-making machinery, neon lights, and polygraph machines (lie detectors). And in 1903, parents and children alike delighted in C. Harold Smith and Edwin Binney's introduction of crayon drawing sticks from their new Crayola Company.

■ NEW REASONING

As the country reinvented itself, academic thinkers around the world proposed startling new scientific theories. In 1905 a Swiss patent clerk named Albert Einstein advanced the theory of relativity. He expressed this theory in a famous equation: $E = mc^2$. Einstein's equation means that energy (E) is equal to an object's mass (m) multiplied by the speed of light (c) squared (multiplied by itself).

Einstein eventually moved to the United States, and his theory turned the world of physics upside down. It told physicists that a very small amount of mass has a huge amount of energy. Einstein's equation proved key to the eventual development of the atom bomb.

■ LOOKING INTO THE MIND

Another European thinker, Austrian physician Sigmund Freud, altered basic assumptions about the psychology of the human mind. Freud emphasized the role of the unconscious mind in human thought and behavior. He introduced radically new and controversial psychological theories about

This **BAKELITE TELEPHONE** was sold to a luxury hotel in Syria. The plastic was also used for items as diverse as radios, kitchen utensils, and airplane parts.

human sexual development and about the way the human psyche (mind and soul) works. In addition, he introduced a therapeutic technique known as psychoanalysis. In this approach, therapists encourage patients to explore their unconscious lives through talking freely about dreams, early childhood, and other personal experiences. Though controversial, Freud attracted many followers, including New York doctor Abraham Brill. Brill studied with Freud and introduced his theories to the United States in 1908 by translating Freud's writings into English. Gradually Freud's theories gained credibility, and the new discipline of psychoanalysis took hold in the United States and around the world. As one doctor wrote to his patient in 1908 about psychoanalysis, "It is likely to have the vogue [popularity] that appendicitis had a decade or so ago."

◾ COFFEE BREAKS

Other theories related to overall human psychological and physical health cropped up as social reformers sought better working conditions for American laborers. For example, the idea of taking a short break from the everyday grind began to gain acceptance in the early 1900s. Historians claim that the idea of an official coffee break began in Buffalo, New York, around 1901. Records from the bygone Larkin Company show that in 1901, employers gave free coffee to their employees. About the same time, another Buffalo business, Barcolo Manufacturing Company, entered coffee break history. According to old newspaper reports, "The employees felt like they needed a mid-morning and mid-afternoon break . . . and one of the employees volunteered to heat the coffee up on a kerosene-fueled hot

Researchers developed both instant and decaffeinated **COFFEE** during the first decade of the 1900s.

Horse carts and streetcars create a **TRAFFIC JAM WITHOUT CARS** in Chicago, Illinois, in 1909.

plate. The employees paid for the coffee . . . and started taking . . . about a 10- to- 15-minute, mid-morning and mid-afternoon coffee break."

■ HORSES, WHEELS, AND ENGINES

To get to work, many Americans took the train. At the beginning of the twentieth century, railroads dominated national and mass travel. Nearly 200,000 miles (321,868 km) of tracks crisscrossed the United States. Many cities still relied on horse-drawn streetcars for public transportation. But in most big cities, people also traveled on cable cars or trolley lines, with Chicago boasting the most extensive system.

Outside cities, life moved at a slower pace. Average families traveled by horse and buggy on potholed, muddy roads. In both the city and the country, transportation changed dramatically during the first decade of the new century.

■ BICYCLES

In the era before cars, bicycles developed into a popular form of transportation. By 1900 more than one million Americans owned bicycles. As bicycles became more affordable, many men, women, and children learned to ride. Bicycles provided greater freedom to an entire generation of women. Until this point in American history, society had frowned upon women going out in public alone. Bicycles permitted women more mobility to go where they wanted when they wanted.

TWO WOMEN WITH BICYCLES wait at a train station in 1906. Critics worried that increased mobility would encourage women to spend too much time away from their families and housework.

Cycling also influenced fashion. New pantslike bloomers and shorter skirts replaced long, heavy skirts, allowing women a greater measure of physical freedom and movement.

Bicycle racing and new bicycle models were popular. Safety bicycles—which had two wheels of equal size instead of one small one in back and one large, high wheel in front—attracted the most attention. The American love affair with bicycles extended to practical matters, such as police patrol. In Long Beach, New York, police chief William Mooney reported that "for street crime, purse snatching, mugging, general malicious mischief, teen trouble areas—[the bicycle is] the most effective police method we've found. It's better than covering an area on foot because our men can get around so fast on bikes."

■ AUTOMOBILES FOR EVERYDAY FOLKS

Several inventors had developed models of automobiles during the late 1890s. They were so expensive, however, that most Americans considered them to be toys for the rich. Cars and the wealthy folks who bought them usually irritated those who were forced to share the same roads. Car owners drove a reckless 10 miles (16 km) per hour. They thoughtlessly forced bicyclists and horse-drawn carriages off bumpy streets. Worse yet, loud rumblings and horn honking from cars scared the horses.

In the opinion of many Americans, cars symbolized all that was wrong with wealthy socialites. Princeton University president and future U.S. president Woodrow Wilson voiced that sentiment when he proclaimed in 1907, "To the countryman, they [automobiles] are a picture of the arrogance of wealth, with all its independence and carelessness."

But into the 1900s, that attitude began to change as automobiles gradually became more affordable. Ransom Olds of Lansing, Michigan, opened Olds Motor Works in 1899. This was the first company to build gasoline-powered automobiles in the United States. The company took an entire year to build four automobiles, which the public chided them would never sell. Olds persisted until 1904. By then his plant was churning out more than five thousand cars annually. Although Olds pioneered automobile production on a larger scale, the "Merry Oldsmobile" still cost too much for most families.

About the same time, Henry Ford, who worked for the Edison Illuminating Company in Detroit, Michigan, was conducting his own automobile experiments after hours. He hoped to create cars that the average family could afford. "I will build a motor car for the great multitude," he said. "It will be large enough for the family, but small enough for the individual to run and care for. . . . But it will be so low in price that no man making a good salary will be unable to own one. . . ."

Taking a gamble, Ford opened the Ford Motor Company in Detroit to build more practical, cheaper cars. The Model A was Ford's first attempt. But this design still cost more than the Oldsmobile.

" I will build a motor car for the great multitude . . . so low in price that no man making a good salary will be unable to own one. . . . "

—*Henry Ford, describing his dream to build an affordable automobile, 1908*

Ford's company looked to other industries for inspiration. At this time, several successful products were being mass produced on assembly lines. For example, Cyrus McCormick manufactured his farm reapers (machines that allowed farmers to harvest crops very quickly) from standard parts that workers assembled piece by piece. Similar forms of assembly production made Isaac Singer's sewing machines and Samuel Colt's revolvers popular and affordable brand names. Even Chicago meatpackers processed beef carcasses by moving them along on overhead conveyor belts.

A Ford engineer decided to take these ideas one step further. He had each worker handle one specific task for assembling a car rather than having teams of workers perform multiple tasks. Ford's workers made the parts and assembled cars, beginning with the frame and adding the rest of the pieces. The resulting assembly line speeded production and reduced costs. In 1908 Ford introduced the Model T for $850. This was $200 less than the average price of a car at that time. Within five years, his staff could produce a car in fewer than six hours, and the price had dropped to half the original cost. William Howard Taft became the first U.S. president to tour the streets in an automobile. More important, the public embraced Ford's new car, which customers proclaimed America's everyman car.

Seeing potential in the expanding automobile industry, competitors entered the market. About fifty start-up companies a year tried to strike it rich. Beginning in 1908, carriage-builder

HENRY FORD demonstrates his Model T car in 1908.

Workers build cars on the **ASSEMBLY LINE** at a Ford factory in 1905.

William Durant began buying out smaller automobile makers, such as Olds, Buick, and Chevrolet. Durant named his new company General Motors, and it became Ford's chief rival for decades to come.

To support the growing auto industry, factories that made gas-powered engines and car parts opened in towns in and around Detroit. Michigan assembly lines supplied the nation and countries overseas with huge numbers of cars. In fact, so many cars came from Michigan that the state earned the nickname Motor Capital of the World.

As automobiles became more affordable, they revolutionized the lifestyle of average American families. Cars provided farmers and small-town folks with the means to make trips to the city, thereby reducing their social isolation. Cars afforded new options for transporting passengers and commercial goods. They also contributed to the growth of suburbs—communities just outside of cities to which families could easily drive. They even generated a new form of leisure activity—car racing.

■ BIRTH OF MODERN AIR TRAVEL

For centuries, men and women around the world had dreamed of flying. In the 1900s, some people tried to fly by attaching birdlike wings to their arms and hurling themselves off rooftops and barns. A few even lived to document and talk about their adventures. Some built gliders with propellers to catch the wind or went up in giant balloons. Into the twentieth century, the pioneer spirit renewed the desire to conquer flight. Adapting the work of those before them, a new crop of trailblazers dabbled with inventions that were both lighter than air—such as balloons—and heavier than air, featuring large, roaring engines.

Between 1900 and 1903, brothers Wilbur and Orville Wright revolutionized travel in heavier-than-air machines by applying scientific principles to mimic the flight of birds. In 1903 their success at Kitty Hawk, North Carolina, at keeping one of their machines airborne for fifty-nine seconds changed history and launched an entire industry. But competition from overseas threatened the Wright brothers' ability to find backers to pay for more research. Still, the Wrights worked to perfect their motorized machine. After five years, the U.S. Army and a French company agreed to give the Wright brothers contracts. By then, they could fly 77 miles (123 km) in almost two and a half hours at more than 40 miles (64 km) per hour.

About the same time that the Wright brothers were conducting their experiments, the U.S. Army took an interest in floating aircraft. Balloons and airships had been in existence since the 1780s, when the French tested the world's first hot-air balloon by filling rubbery silk with hydrogen, the lightest of gases, to make it rise. Since then large, round balloons had been used for sport riding and to test weather conditions. Longer, sausage-shaped balloons called dirigibles had frames large enough to hold passengers—a possibility that Europeans were exploring.

In 1907 the U.S. Army bought two hydrogen balloons. Officers practiced flying the balloons for a few months. The army liked the balloons and purchased a framed dirigible for its Signal Corps (an army branch responsible for communications) to test. By 1908 the army had built its own airship. The new machines and the government team that cared for them formed the foundation of the future U.S. Air Force.

An army officer tests a **HYDROGEN BALLOON** in 1907.

THE WRIGHT BROTHERS tested their glider by flying it like a kite. In this 1901 picture, Wilbur stands at the left and Orville at the right.

A major breakthrough in the science of flight came from two Dayton, Ohio, brothers—Wilbur and Orville Wright. The Wright brothers repaired and built bicycles for a living. But their dream remained tackling air travel. The two studied everything already written about gliders and researched engines, elevators, and air pressure. The most helpful information, however, came from watching buzzards fly.

One problem with earlier gliders was the inability to control rolling (the tendency of gliders to flip upside down). The Wrights discovered that when thrown off course by the wind, buzzards stayed upright by adjusting one of their wings up or down. This movement by one wing corrected air pressure under the other wing. Perhaps, the Wrights reasoned, pulling a wing tip up or down would keep a glider from rolling too.

The Wrights first tried their idea with a kite. Then, in 1900, they built a glider to test on a beach near Kitty Hawk, North Carolina. At first, their success was limited. But over the next two years, the brothers experimented with ever longer and sleeker wing shapes until they found a design that stayed airborne. After almost one thousand glides, they added a four-cylinder gasoline engine. The brothers secured the engine to the glider with bicycle chains and returned to Kitty Hawk in 1903 for another test run. On December 14, Wilbur propelled the glider barely 60 feet (18 meters) before crashing.

His brother refused to give up. Three days later, Orville positioned himself next to the engine on the lower wing. After a shaky takeoff, the glider flew 120 feet (36 meters) for twelve seconds. Hours later, Wilbur tried again. This time he stayed in the air for fifty-nine seconds and flew 852 feet (259 meters)—a world record. A surprised onlooker yelled, "They have done it! Damned if they ain't flew!"

45

SWITCHBOARD OPERATORS connect calls in New York City around 1901. At the time, rural areas typically had only one switchboard to handle all calls.

■ COMMUNICATION

The United States in the early 1900s lacked modern forms of mass communication such as the Internet and television. Speakers who wanted to champion a cause spread their message by traveling from city to city to make speeches in public halls and to sell brochures they had self-published. Only about 2 percent of Americans owned telephones. Their calls went through switchboard operators, who had to physically connect wires to allow calls to be completed and who could also listen to the conversations and learn everyone's business. Most long-distance communication meant writing a letter that took days or weeks to reach its destination.

During the late nineteenth century, the U.S. Post Office Department (the predecessor of the U.S. Postal Service) experimented with several ways to connect people in different parts of the country easily and quickly. In 1901 the Post Office Department contracted to carry mail by horseless carriage (the era's term for automobile) between the post office in Buffalo, New York, and the city's

Pan-American Exposition grounds. The 4.5-mile (7.2 km) car trip took thirty-five minutes. Administrators were so pleased with this speedy drive that they expanded the program to deliver mail from 454 post offices around the country. Between 1901 and 1914, the post office arranged for all mail delivery to be contracted to various automobile services.

Rural homes were difficult to reach by car. With only 150 miles (241 km) of paved roads in the entire United States, most farms were unreachable except by horse and buggy. Farmers often traveled great distances to the nearest post office to retrieve their mail. As the push for free home delivery of mail mounted, local communities urged lawmakers to extend and build a network of better roads and highways. Between 1897 and 1908, local governments spent about $72 million on bridges, drain pipes, and road paving. As a result, millions of Americans in rural areas received the same free mail service as did larger manufacturing centers.

A POSTAL WORKER DELIVERS MAIL BY HORSE-DRAWN SLEIGH to a farm in south central Minnesota around 1910. Harsh weather complicated mail delivery in many areas of the United States.

HOMESTEAD STEEL WORKS in Homestead, Pennsylvania, was one of the steel factories acquired by U.S. Steel in 1901. It would become the most productive steel factory in the world.

Chapter Four

BIG BUSINESS AND WORKERS' RIGHTS:
The 1900s Economy

W hen Theodore Roosevelt entered the White House, barely 1 percent of the American population were millionaires. Yet millionaires owned 20 percent of the nation's wealth. A small number of wealthy men dominated U.S. business and industry, and most felt they were entitled to whatever wealth they accumulated.

Many American millionaires ran giant corporations. These corporations often forced smaller companies out of business, took them over, and formed larger businesses called trusts. A few politicians wanted to pass laws called antitrust regulations to prevent corporations from forcing out competitors. But most millionaires were against such laws.

Corporation owners believed they had the right to run their businesses as they pleased. They also believed that their responsibilities lay with their businesses—not with smaller companies or with society as a whole. "I owe the public nothing," declared John Pierpont Morgan, a millionaire financier responsible for the merger that created corporate giant U.S. Steel.

Roosevelt bristled at this attitude. He wasn't against big business. He just wanted more government controls that took the average citizen into account. As president, Roosevelt took steps to control big business by invoking the 1890 Sherman Anti-Trust Act. He used this antitrust regulation to dissolve Morgan's Northern Securities Company monopoly. The company had combined several railroad firms into one trust that controlled all train travel between the Great Lakes and the Pacific Coast of the United States. The decision to break up the monopoly was controversial and went all the way to the U.S. Supreme Court. In a 5–4 decision in 1904, the Court agreed with Roosevelt to break up the monopoly. The decision alerted American millionaire tycoons that business as usual was about to change.

Roosevelt was the first of three U.S. presidents to champion such progressive causes. But his impact on big business proved to be limited. When Taft became president after Roosevelt, he launched his own attack against large trusts as part of a bid for support from progressives. In fact, Taft wound up spearheading more antitrust lawsuits than Roosevelt. This became Taft's main achievement during his presidency.

This 1901 cartoon shows **JOHN PIERPONT MORGAN** as a menacing bull blowing "Wall Street bubbles" chased by financiers and ordinary people alike. Tycoons like Morgan grew more and more unpopular with the public as they fought to maintain their business monopolies.

■ ASSEMBLY LINES

The American workplace was changing rapidly in the early 1900s. At one time in U.S. labor history, a single worker produced a product from beginning to end. By the beginning of the 1900s, most employees were working on assembly lines in large factories or were taking parts of products home to assemble. More often, jobs involved attaching one part to another as a product moved along a conveyor belt. Humans became cogs in manufacturing wheels. Work was monotonous, pay was by the piece, and hours were long with few if any employee benefits. The pride of crafting a finished product from beginning to end disappeared.

■ NEW COMPANY TOWNS

As the nation grew, entire cities developed around specific industries. For example, until 1905 the area that became Gary, Indiana, consisted of barren sand dunes covered with scrub brushes. That year Judge Elbert Gary, who was the chairperson of the U.S. Steel Corporation's governing board, declared his district the site of a new steel-processing development. "We'll build near the railroad junction of Chicago, where

Humans became cogs in manufacturing wheels. . . . The pride of crafting a finished product from beginning to end disappeared.

acres of land can be had almost for the asking, midway between the ore regions of the North and the coal regions of the South and East," he said. By 1910 the new town of Gary, Indiana, had been born. It boasted huge smoke-belching steel mills and foundries, a harbor for ore boats, a railroad station, and a population of almost seventeen thousand people.

Many of these towns belonged to the companies that built them. Everything—homes, schools, and stores—was controlled by business owners, who lived far from town. People who worked and lived in the towns gave their salaries back to the company through rent and payment for supplies. Between the high prices that company stores charged for goods and the long hours of dangerous work the companies demanded of their employees, many workers in these "company towns" were no better off than their counterparts in crowded inner-city slums.

No matter where workers lived, most felt exploited by their employers. American factory workers in 1900 generally earned an average of only $490 a year, which even at that time was not a living wage. One in eight Americans nationwide lived in poverty, and poor Americans died at twice the rate of those who were better off. Unmoved by the hardships that imbalances in the distribution of wealth could cause, one wealthy man vowed, "We own America; we got it, God knows how, but we intend to keep it."

■ WORKERS PUSH FOR RIGHTS

American workers had long realized that if reform were to occur, it had to come from them. No matter how hard presidents Roosevelt and Taft pushed, American financiers still wielded too much power. Legislators (lawmakers) refused to make significant changes that would force wealthy business owners to be more accountable to workers. Even language in the Sherman Anti-Trust Act was turned against employees trying to gain basic rights. Throughout the decade, courts conspired with big business by agreeing that worker groups, such as unions, were "illegal combinations

MINERS TAKE A DINNER BREAK more than 2 miles (3.2 km) below ground in an Illinois coal mine around 1903. Many miners worked without seeing daylight for weeks at a time. Most were deeply in debt to their employers.

in restraint of trade"—a phrase originally written into the Sherman Act to describe monopolies and trusts.

In 1902 employees from D. E. Loewe & Co. of Danbury, Connecticut, wanted the United Hatters Union to represent them as a closed shop (a workplace in which all the workers are unionized). But Loewe & Co. refused to accept unionization. Workers protested with a walkout (refusal to stay on the job), but it failed. In response, employees waged a boycott of Loewe products, refusing to buy the hats the company produced. The boycott cost the company almost

	1900s	2000s (first decade)
Average U.S. worker's yearly income	$862	$35,000

Typical Prices

Candy bar	5¢	75¢
Bottle of soda	5¢	$1.00
Loaf of bread	4¢	$2.79
Quart of milk	6¢	$1.79
Gallon of gas	10¢	$2.80
Movie ticket	5¢	$9.00
Man's haircut	25¢	$30.00
Pair of men's shoes	$13.00	$79.99
Child's bicycle	$50.00	$139.99
Two-door car	$825	$20,000
Three-bedroom house	$2,400	$300,000

(Prices are samples only. At any given time, prices vary by year, location, size, brand, and model.)

one hundred thousand dollars in lost sales. Loewe fought back with a successful lawsuit against the union. The suit claimed the boycott restricted trade under the Sherman Act.

Another misuse of the act occurred against the American Federation of Labor (AFL), a major organization for workers' rights. One tool the AFL used to educate its members was to list antiunion companies in its publication the *American Federationist.* In 1907 Buck's Stove and Range Company, a stove manufacturer that had been involved in a labor dispute with its employees, challenged the AFL over listing the firm in its publication. Buck's arranged for a court order to prevent the listing on the grounds that such filings caused restraint of trade.

SAMUEL GOMPERS was born in London, England, and trained as a cigar maker. He became president of the AFL union in 1886.

AFL president Samuel Gompers responded by blasting the court in a newspaper editorial. He wrote: "Until a law is passed making it compulsory upon [required for] labor men to buy stoves, we need not buy them, we won't buy them, and we will persuade other fair-minded, sympathetic friends of labor to cooperate with us and leave the blamed things alone." Several courts struck down the stove boycott, dealing another blow to workers.

■ UNSKILLED WORKERS UNITE

In the early 1900s, the American labor movement was in its infancy. The AFL was the first group to assemble workers on a large scale to fight for better working conditions. Under Gompers's leadership, the AFL created a national organization of unions that were organized by craft. (Common crafts at the time included bricklaying, printing, and tailoring.) Federation leaders kept out of politics. Instead, they pushed for peaceful discussions between their representatives and employers to bring about changes in individual company working conditions. Although gains were limited, membership increased from 550,000 to 2 million between 1900 and 1910.

Even with increasing membership, many members felt disappointed with the slow progress of the AFL. And because the AFL was oriented toward craft workers, unskilled workers could not join. Whole groups of employees went without union representation. Many American workers felt that only a complete shakeup of labor could bring justice to the American labor force. For that reason, forty-three groups of discontented American labor leaders assembled the Industrial Workers of the World (IWW) in Chicago, Illinois, in 1905. The IWW, also called the Wobblies, gave hope to activist workers whose voices had often been ignored. Leading IWW supporters included immigrant and activist Mary "Mother" Jones, political rabble-rouser Eugene Debs, and labor organizer Lucy Parsons, who supported an eight-hour workday (as opposed to the much longer workdays many Americans endured in the early 1900s). Yet because so many different voices in the American labor movement were pushing so many different agendas, the IWW took a few years to sort out unified goals and direction.

In the early 1900s, Big Bill Haywood, who had started working in Nevada mines at the age of fifteen, took charge of the IWW's squabbling group of six thousand members. The IWW drew its membership from lumberjacks, migrant farmworkers, plains cowboys, and hoboes. Haywood had dabbled in many jobs, from mining to bronco busting to homesteading, so he understood the perspectives and concerns of many different types of workers.

From the beginning, the major thrust of the IWW was its members' battle for free speech. Although the U.S. Constitution protects free speech, police still sometimes arrested workers for holding street meetings and attending protests. In support of workers' free-speech rights, the IWW free-speech fighters rode the rails to wherever laborers needed to be heard. Then they organized public meetings for the laborers, often getting arrested on purpose in hopes of calling attention to workers' rights.

In 1908 the IWW went to Spokane, Washington, to help lumberjacks

WILLIAM D. "BIG BILL" HAYWOOD worked to create the IWW—a single, united union that represented workers in many different businesses.

there speak out against employment agents who were exploiting them. Lumberjacks often moved to different lumber camps throughout the year, depending on which camps had jobs to offer them. For a sizable fee, employment agents offered to match workers with camps that they claimed were in need of workers. Workers had little choice but to pay the fee, as employment agents were their only source for finding jobs in an era with no computers and few telephones. When the workers trudged to the next camp, however, they often found that the boss had no work to offer. Other times, the boss might hire workers for only a day or two before firing them on flimsy charges. The lumberjacks were left without a job and no way to reclaim the fee.

When the IWW arrived in Spokane, it sent out calls for workers to attend peaceful rallies, speak to the crowd, and expect to be jailed for making those speeches. The idea was to fill the city's jails and wear down the police. The call was successful. One after another, speakers mounted the soapbox (that

Anarchist activist Alexander Berkman speaks to **WORKERS AT AN IWW RALLY** in New York City in 1908. The IWW brought together people from urban and rural areas, with different cultures and philosophies, to improve workplace conditions.

Before speakers could even finish a sentence, the police yanked them off to jail.

is, they gave impromptu speeches before the crowd, using a soapbox as their platform). Before speakers could even finish a sentence, the police yanked them off to jail. After arresting 103 speakers, the police grew weary. The last man to climb on the soapbox began with, "Friends and fellow workers . . ." and stopped. He fully expected to be hauled off by police. When they didn't appear, he panicked. He never thought he would have to say anything past opening remarks.

Fortunately for the speaker, the protest ended shortly thereafter. The protesters felt that the rally had been a success, and they began to disperse. But in spite of the rally's success, employment agents' unfair practices continued throughout the early 1900s. The practices proved difficult to stop with even the most effective protest tactics.

■ "WE WANT TIME TO PLAY"

One of the most troubling work issues of the decade involved child labor. In 1900 more than 2.2 million American children under the age of sixteen worked instead of attending school. Children worked in many different industries, but textile mills and other factories employed the greatest number of young weavers, spinners, and janitors. Most children earned less than twenty-five cents a day, which their families desperately needed to survive.

A smattering of state laws technically limited the age at which children could begin working and also defined the number of hours they could work each day. But few employers paid attention to these laws—and with little negative consequence. Families often lied about their children's ages so they could get jobs and bring home additional income. Companies preferred the cheap labor. In fact, some bosses threatened to fire or evict parents from company-owned houses if they refused to let their children work.

In 1903 Philadelphia's Central Textile Workers Union insisted that the city's millowners reduce the workweek from sixty-five to fifty-five hours. When the mills refused, one hundred thousand textile workers left area factories in what the *Philadelphia Inquirer* called the "largest known" textile strike. (A strike is a stoppage of work to try to force companies to meet a union's demands.)

A YOUNG MILL WORKER pauses in her work at a spinning machine in 1908. Cotton manufacturers preferred child workers for this task because they could reach the spun threads easily with their small fingers.

"Mother" Jones, aged seventy-three at the time, went to Philadelphia to help arrange worker meetings and peaceful demonstrations. She was appalled when she discovered that about sixteen thousand of the strikers were maimed and bedraggled children. Jones asked journalists why they never wrote about these child workers. Reporters told her that many millowners also held stock (financial shares) in the newspapers, so the reporters were forced to censor (limit coverage of) what went into print. "Well, I've got stock in these children, and I'll arrange a little publicity," Jones countered.

Jones proceeded to organize demonstrations against child labor. She gave speeches, pointing out the broken bones and stooped backs of young workers. She described the worn bodies of child workers as sacrifices on the altars of greedy profiteers. Her gatherings attracted crowds that newspapers couldn't ignore.

While the efforts of Jones and other American labor leaders went a long way in the quest to gain more rights for U.S. workers, they were not a cure-all. Newspaper articles about Jones's demonstrations

" I've got stock in these children. "

—Mary "Mother" Jones, speaking of the child laborers for whom she worked and organized, 1903

drew attention to labor issues. But labor practices were hard to change, and workers continued to grapple with hardships such as child labor and low wages throughout the early 1900s and beyond.

On July 7, 1903, Mary "Mother" Jones took a group of nearly two hundred child laborers—as well as one hundred adult textile workers—on a 125-mile (200 km), twenty-two-day march from the Liberty Bell in Philadelphia to President Roosevelt's family summer home in Oyster Bay on Long Island, New York. Jones hoped to convince the president of the need for national child labor laws so the marchers could attend school and play at the beach like his own children.

The children carried U.S. flags and signs that read, "We Want Time to Play" and "We Only Ask for Justice." Jones marched alongside the group in her trademark black hat and long, black dress with a white-trimmed collar. Her sense of purpose showed in her businesslike stride, straight back, and firm, bespectacled expression.

Supporters along the way donated food and lodging to the ragtag group of pale-faced, skinny marchers. When they neared the state of New Jersey, a Princeton University professor invited Jones to speak to his class. She arrived with a haggard and stooped ten-year-old boy marcher in tow. "Here's a textbook on economics," she began, pointing to her sidekick. "He gets three dollars a week and his sister who is fourteen gets six dollars. They work in a carpet factory ten hours a day while the children of the rich are getting higher education." The professor never expected Jones to challenge the system so vividly.

MOTHER JONES leads hundreds of child laborers in a 1903 march for child labor laws.

Nor did President Roosevelt, who ultimately refused to see the marchers. Roosevelt issued a statement asserting that the passage of laws limiting child labor was up to individual states.

Although many were disappointed that Roosevelt refused to see Jones and her marchers, Jones was content to have made her point. Through her efforts, the American public could see up close the evils of hiring children, and the topic wasn't going to go away. Two years later, Pennsylvania legislators passed a bill that limited child labor. Other states followed with tougher child-labor laws. Jones and her marchers ultimately helped to spur what became the Fair Labor Standards Act of 1938—which, among other things, limited the types of jobs that children could perform and required employers to pay child workers at least the minimum wage.

IMMIGRANT STONECARVERS FROM ITALY pose with their work on the site of the State Historical Society building in Madison, Wisconsin, around 1910.

Chapter Five

BATTLING INEQUALITY:
Immigrants, Minorities, and Women

Many new immigrants arrived in the United States at the beginning of the twentieth century. Between 1900 and 1910 alone, more than 14.1 million people passed through immigration centers in San Francisco, New York, and Seattle. Unlike in previous periods of immigration from northern and western Europe, newcomers to the United States in the early 1900s tended to come from southern and eastern European nations such as Italy, Austria, Russia, and Hungary. They tended to be white and practice a range of religions, including Judaism, Catholicism, or Eastern Orthodox Christianity. The largest numbers of immigrants were Italians. Shortages of food, land, and jobs in Italy had triggered the move for this group, while political and religious freedom attracted refugees from eastern Europe and Russia. In contrast, the earlier flow of Asian immigrants into the United States had slowed to a trickle due to quota laws limiting their numbers.

Most immigrants settled in large cities, including New York, Chicago, Cleveland, Milwaukee, Detroit, and Buffalo. With limited English and undeveloped job skills, they often took low-paying, unskilled jobs or factory work—mainly in machine shops and garment factories. Other immigrant families opened cleaners, newsstands, and grocery stores. But without high-paying jobs, most new arrivals could only afford to live in cramped apartments or houses in dirty, overcrowded neighborhoods.

The large number of immigrants changed the face of U.S. cities, creating new neighborhoods of similar ethnic populations, such as Little Italy in New York City. Because immigrants faced discrimination from American society at large, they stayed close to other immigrants from the same homeland. They were often excluded socially from mainstream society. So immigrant groups organized their own clubs and religious institutions. They even raised money to buy cemeteries where they could be buried together.

Newcomers experienced continual challenges. As recent immigrants to the United States, they accepted lower wages and worked longer hours to get a start in their new homeland. This created tensions between them and more settled immigrant groups. Recent arrivals were viewed as spoilers who competed for jobs and undercut ongoing attempts to gain higher wages and better

Immigrant women and children sew clothing in their **CROWDED TENEMENT APARTMENT** in New York City around 1905. Sewing and doing laundry were common ways that women could make money to support themselves and their families.

working conditions. The "No Irish Need Apply" signs that had once hung outside many businesses were replaced with signs that read, "No Jews (or Italians) Need Apply."

As tensions over immigration grew, the U.S. government passed a series of new laws to limit entry into the country and to allow officials to deport (send back home) newcomers more easily. In 1903, for example, after President McKinley's assassination, immigration laws allowed officials to deport anyone who advocated the overthrow of the U.S. government. Two bills extended previous Chinese exclusion acts and gave the president authority to refuse admission to certain nationalities believed to hurt labor conditions in the United States. Other laws expanded the list of what would disqualify someone from being admitted into the United States. For example, immigrants were subjected to new physical and mental health evaluations.

Immigrants were eager to build new lives for themselves in the United States. But as immigration increased, so did the conflicts between established U.S. residents and those just beginning to gain a foothold in the country.

In spite of increased restrictions on immigration, the numbers of newcomers settling in the United States continued to grow. Immigrants were eager to build new lives for themselves in the United States. But as immigration increased, so did the conflicts between established U.S. residents and those just beginning to gain a foothold in the country.

■ IMMIGRATION AND HEALTH

In 1900 tensions between new immigrants and longtime U.S. citizens came to a head over an unexpected issue—health. In the summer of that year, bubonic plague hit the densely crowded Chinatown community in San Francisco. People who got sick suffered headaches, vomiting, and high fevers before eventually dying of the disease. Prejudice against Asian immigrants gripped white Americans. Whites often blamed Asians for spreading the deadly sickness. The mayor of San Francisco tried to contain the panic—and illness—by shutting off Chinatown and its twenty thousand residents from the rest of the city. Police scoured the area to find and remove sick residents. But they allowed whites to pass freely in and out of Chinatown.

63

SAN FRANCISCO'S CHINATOWN became the largest Chinese community outside of China.

Chinatown residents complained that, as a result of the police action, businesses were losing a considerable amount of money. They also worried that fearful whites would purposely poison their water supply. Indeed, some white officials wanted to burn down Chinatown to eliminate disease. President McKinley responded to officials' fears by calling for a quarantine (restriction on movement) of all Asian residents in San Francisco. Asians were not permitted to travel on trains leaving the city unless they had obtained health certificates from the Marine Hospital Service (the forerunner of the U.S. Public Health Service). The quarantine was eventually challenged in federal court, where it was declared unconstitutional.

In 1901 officials began a cleanup effort in Chinatown. They thoroughly cleansed about twelve hundred houses. Shortly thereafter, illnesses diminished for a time—but they reemerged again around 1907. By then evidence was mounting that flea-carrying rats spread the plague. Officials offered a reward for finding and killing rats. The rat-catching campaign was a success. But the pain and fear caused by racism during the plague left a lasting impact on San Francisco's Chinese Americans.

■ NATIVE AMERICANS

Immigrants were not the only ones who faced discrimination in the early 1900s. Native Americans also suffered the effects of racial prejudice in the United States. After resettling entire Native American nations onto reservations in the mid-1800s, U.S. government bureaucrats hoped to "humanize and civilize [Native Americans] . . . into hard-working Christian taxpayers." They decided that the easiest way to do this was to focus on Native American children—the future of Native American communities.

Reformers decided to set up separate schools for Native American children. These schools would be boarding schools (schools at which meals and lodging are provided), and they would be located miles away from the children's homes and communities. Eager reformers tore Native American children ages six to sixteen from their families and placed them in the schools. Everything about the schools was designed to wipe out the children's Native American heritage. Students weren't allowed to have long hair (an important cultural tradition for many Native Americans). Instead of traditional clothing, the children had to wear Victorian-style uniforms consisting of long dresses for girls and pants and jackets for boys. They also had to give up their traditional footwear in favor of stiff shoes and stockings.

Children were expected to speak and think only in English and not in their own languages. They were taught the value of individual wealth and property—ideals not recognized in Native American communities. Teachers told the students that Christopher Columbus had discovered America even though the

NATIVE AMERICAN BOYS AT THE CARLISLE INDIAN SCHOOL in Pennsylvania learned skills such as shoemaking. Reformers hoped that the boys would get jobs that would keep them away from their traditional lifestyle.

children's ancestors had been there long before Columbus arrived in the 1400s. Teachers also forced their Native American students to pledge allegiance to the U.S. flag, which represented the people who had brutally conquered them.

As reform intensified, Native American children were required to attend Christian church services and Sunday school. Anyone who protested received physical punishment. Many children were psychologically abused. Teachers told the students that their culture was savage and inferior.

Some experts of the day realized that the boarding schools were harming Native American students. They urged teachers in such schools to respect the students' cultures and beliefs. For instance, psychologist and educator expert G. Stanley Hall encouraged instructors to "build on an Indian child's natural capacities and background rather than obliterate them." He preferred that teachers "make [the students] good Indian[s] rather than a cheap imitation of the white man." In spite of such urging, abuses continued in the boarding schools. And although the schools were failing in their mission, the U.S. government did not begin to close them until the 1920s.

Many children were psychologically abused. Teachers told them that their culture was savage and inferior.

■ AFRICAN AMERICANS UNDER FIRE

African Americans also faced racial struggles. By 1900 almost nine million African Americans lived in the United States, mostly in the South. African Americans were the majority population in South Carolina and Mississippi. Almost 50 percent of the population in Georgia and Louisiana was African American. At that time, many whites feared that African Americans would take control of the South if they gained political power there. For that reason, many southern states devised a host of Jim Crow laws to restrict various economic, physical, and political freedoms of African Americans.

The label "Jim Crow" originated from a character of the same name who became popular in the 1830s through racist white minstrel (variety show) entertainer Thomas Dartmouth Rice. Rice blackened his face and danced onstage as a bungling black person named Jim Crow. As the African American community in the United States grew, whites throughout the South passed more Jim Crow laws. Because

AN AFRICAN AMERICAN FARMER PLOWS HIS FIELD in Virginia around 1901.
By 1910 hundreds of thousands of African Americans supported themselves with
farming. But they still faced discrimination. In the South, whites sometimes used
Jim Crow laws to take away farms belonging to African Americans.

of these restrictions, many African Americans built separate communities. Many
of these communities thrived, offering livelihoods for a growing black middle
class and electing several African Americans to the U.S. Congress.

Jim Crow laws continued in full force throughout the first half of the 1900s,
as majority white society became increasingly threatened by expanding black
political power. Slowly, legalized discrimination whittled away freedoms African Americans had gained immediately after the Civil War (1861–1865). Towns
across the South passed laws to prevent African Americans from buying property, voting, being recognized in courts, and using the same schools, bathrooms,
water fountains, restaurants, and hotels as whites. Increasingly, African Americans were forced to use separate doors to enter public buildings, including hospi-
tals, and to remove their hats or step off sidewalks when a white person crossed
their path. In Louisiana alone, the number of voting African Americans dropped
from 130,334 in 1894 to 1,342 in 1904 because of new voting laws that made it
almost impossible for blacks in the South to vote.

African Americans in many areas of the United States faced violent hostil-
ity. For example, they were often subjected to lynchings (deaths by hanging).

Townspeople pose with the body of **A MAN LYNCHED IN LAWRENCEVILLE, GEORGIA,** after he was accused of assaulting a white woman around 1910.

More African Americans were lynched in the first two decades of the twentieth century than in any other time in U.S. history.

African American men and teenage boys were lynched more often than women or girls. The typical pattern was for an un-named source to leak informa-tion that an African American male seemed to be too familiar with a white woman. That night a band of white thugs (often members of the Ku Klux Klan, a white supremacy group) would come to lynch the boy or man. This murderous action sometimes resulted from a simple sideways glance at a white woman. Usually, a prejudiced white with a grudge faked the claim of an offense.

The 1905 novel *The Clansman: An Historical Romance of the Ku Klux Klan* by southerner Thomas Dixon fueled the flames of racial hatred. The novel height-ened fears among southerners about out-of-control freedmen (former slaves) threatening the safety of white families. The book's popularity—and later, its adaptation into a movie—planted the seeds for expanding the Ku Klux Klan.

ACHIEVING SUCCESS

In this atmosphere of racial tension, two African American women, Madam C. J. Walker and Maggie Lena Walker (no relation), started businesses that made them unusual in any U.S. community. At this time, women rarely ran big busi-nesses. Born in Louisiana, Madam Walker turned her homemade hair care prod-ucts into a national business. She opened a factory, salons, and training school for hundreds of saleswomen. By 1910 Walker had become the first female mil-lionaire, black or white, in the United States.

A portrait of **MADAM C. J. WALKER** appeared on the packaging for her popular vegetable shampoo in 1906.

Maggie Walker originally taught public school in Richmond, Virginia. But the district forced her to quit after she married (a common practice at the time). Walker turned her attention to promoting African American businesses through a religious organization called the Independent Order of Saint Luke. Her business skills strengthened the order's finances enough to open a bank and a store, start a newspaper, and spread the order's resources into twenty-two states. In 1903 Walker opened the Saint Luke Penny Savings Bank in Richmond, Virginia, becoming the first woman bank president in the United States. Saint Luke's was Richmond's only African American-owned bank, and it is the nation's longest-running bank owned by African Americans that is still in operation.

Self-made African Americans distinguished themselves in every profession. One of the most famous African American leaders of the era was

" Invest in the human soul. Who knows, it may be a diamond in the rough. "

—Mary McLeod Bethune, African American educator (1875–1955)

Booker T. Washington. Washington, who was born a slave on a Virginia plantation in 1856, worked his way through Hampton Normal and Agricultural Institute (a college) as a janitor. He then helped to found Tuskegee Institute in Alabama, turning it into a respected center for higher education for African Americans.

Washington's attitude toward race relations was not to make waves. He believed that self-improvement and hard work within the system would breed success for African Americans, as it had for him. Eventually, Washington emphasized, education and economic independence would allow African Americans to overcome Jim Crow laws. This philosophy endeared him to the nation's white leaders, including industrialists such as Andrew Carnegie, who contributed to the Tuskegee Institute. Speaking in Atlanta, Georgia, in 1895, Washington said, "The wisest among my race understand that the agitation of questions of social equality is the extremist folly. . . ."

President Roosevelt recognized Washington as a powerful African American leader. In 1901 he invited Washington to the White House to discuss key issues for African American voters. After their discussion, Roosevelt welcomed Washington to dine with him. Washington was the first African American to receive that honor. Reporters publicized the dinner, causing an uproar among southern congressional representatives. Relations between that group of lawmakers and the White House soured for the rest of Roosevelt's term. Because of this political pressure, Roosevelt never invited Washington to the White House again.

■ MOVES TO COMBAT RACISM

Not all African Americans shared Washington's patience to wait for the world to improve. In Georgia, Atlanta University sociology professor W. E. B. DuBois worried that long-term submission to whites was crushing African American manhood. DuBois, the first African American to earn a PhD from Harvard, advocated bolder tactics to achieve equal rights.

In 1905 DuBois organized a secret meeting of twenty-nine African American leaders in Niagara Falls, Ontario, in Canada. The leaders criticized Washington's policy of refusing to advocate more forcefully for change. They began calling themselves the Niagara Movement. They created a manifesto (statement

W. E. B DUBOIS fought for racial equality, freedom of speech, and humane working conditions for African Americans for more than sixty years. This portrait was taken in 1904.

n 1906 racism led to an ugly incident in the city of Brownsville, Texas. The incident sprang from tensions between the white citizens of Brownsville and African American infantrymen (foot soldiers) stationed at a military post nearby. The infantrymen had distinguished themselves during the Spanish-American War and in the Philippines. Yet the Brownsville community had subjected the men to discrimination from the day they first arrived.

Early in the morning of August 14, a fight took place in Brownsville. A police officer was injured in the fight. A white bartender was killed. Although it had been dark when the fight took place, residents claimed that they had seen the infantrymen on the scene. The residents blamed the African American soldiers for the white bartender's death.

Twelve soldiers were arrested as a result of the Brownsville incident. They insisted that they were innocent, and no damaging evidence emerged. But officials believed the white witnesses, and the soldiers were charged with disobedience for their refusal to confess.

Niagara Movement lawyers tried to help the soldiers. But after a white woman falsely charged an African American soldier with rape, President Roosevelt closed the fort and moved to discharge all 167 infantrymen.

The dishonorable discharge ruined the soldiers' lives. It deprived them of pay and left them without any pensions (payments made to soldiers and workers after they have retired). Only Senator Joseph Foraker of Ohio defended the soldiers in Congress. But the decision was never reversed.

In 1972 evidence confirmed that the twelve soldiers had been framed. President Richard Nixon signed a bill to reverse the dishonorable discharges and to pay the sole survivor twenty-five thousand dollars.

71

of beliefs) that declared: "We claim for ourselves every single right that belongs to a freeborn American, political, civil and social; and until we get these rights we will never cease to protest and assail [attack] the ears of America."

At about this same time, in August 1908, a race riot broke out in Springfield, Illinois. Someone had falsely accused an African American man of sexually assaulting a white woman. The charge triggered two days of violent attacks by whites against African Americans in that city. The Illinois governor called in the state militia (troops) to stop the raging mob. In the end, two elderly African American men were lynched, several people were shot, and homes and stores throughout the African American community were burned and looted.

After the riot, whites who supported African American rights began to fear that the country was sliding backward in race relations. Activist and writer Mary White Ovington approached DuBois about creating a mixed-race group to combat the rising racial violence. As a result, DuBois and other progressives founded the National Association for the Advancement of Colored People (NAACP). DuBois's Niagara Movement disbanded in 1910—but many of its members joined the NAACP to take up the call for the civil and political liberties of all races.

■ WOMEN SPEAK OUT

Like African Americans, women battled severe inequalities in the early 1900s. Conditions for women had improved somewhat from earlier generations. But women's rights varied greatly depending upon where a woman lived and which state laws applied there. American women in the 1900s had a long way to go to achieve true equality with men.

Common wisdom of the era claimed that women needed protection. Their head-to-toe clothing reflected the sheltering that American society felt they required. According to one historian discussing the times, "The best—and safest—thing for a girl to do was to sit at home and help her mother about the house and wait for the 'right man.'"

A man's job was to accompany his wife or daughter everywhere. This requirement was thought necessary to safeguard her reputation and physical well-being. Unmarried females were never to venture outdoors on their own in the city. Instead, a male family member or a maid accompanied the woman to ensure that she was treated with respect. If a man had a private encounter with a girlfriend or stole a kiss, everyone assumed he wanted her hand in marriage.

Washington and eight other states even passed bills meant to protect a woman's honor. For example, Washington State passed a law in 1909 making it illegal to speak any false or dishonoring words that would cast doubt on a female's virtue and chastity. Such laws were known as virtue laws.

According to one historian, "The best—and safest—thing for a girl to do was to sit at home and help her mother about the house and wait for the 'right man.'"

CARRIE CHAPMAN CATT makes a call from her office around 1909.

Many early activists believed conditions would improve dramatically for women if only they could get the right to vote. Carrie Chapman Catt was one such activist. Catt was born in Ripon, Wisconsin, in 1859. She attended Iowa State Agricultural College in Ames, Iowa, and began her career as a teacher and journalist. Catt joined the Iowa woman suffrage (voting rights) movement in the late 1880s. State leaders noticed her ability to hold an audience and organize people for a cause.

Catt quickly rose through the ranks of national suffrage leadership, first organizing clubs and eventually serving as a delegate at the convention of the National American Woman Suffrage Association (NAWSA). In 1900, when fellow activist Susan B. Anthony retired from her position as NAWSA's president, she passed the gavel to Catt.

Catt gave NAWSA the foundation to build a winning movement. She prepared a manual of operation for the group and raised considerable funds to help promote its cause. Catt's major achievement involved extending the NAWSA into southern states, which was considered a revolutionary move.

In 1904 Catt resigned as president to nurse her sick husband. But she resumed her role at NAWSA's helm in time to see the 1920 passage of constitutional amendment nineteen—the amendment giving women the right to vote.

73

■ WOMEN AND THE LAW

Despite virtue laws, women settlers in western states generally enjoyed similar rights to men—although they didn't yet have the right to vote. The harsh conditions of pioneer life in the West required that everyone in the family pitch in equally. Since women and men worked side by side, state constitutions in the western United States largely supported women's rights.

On the East Coast, the situation was different. Women had gained the right to own property and keep any wages that they earned (as opposed to having to give all earnings to their husbands). But eastern states enacted other laws to limit female independence. For example, a married woman in Pennsylvania needed her husband's approval to sign a business contract. In some states, women could be arrested if caught smoking. Or they could be banned from staying in a hotel or eating at a restaurant if they tried to do so without an escort.

Women in southern states had even fewer rights than their counterparts to the north. In Louisiana, men held legal rights to everything a woman owned, including the clothes on her back. Fewer white women worked outside the home in the South than in other parts of the country. In Georgia those who did turned over all wages to their husbands.

Almost all states discriminated against women when it came to divorce—and divorce was not widely accepted to begin with. If a woman divorced in Minnesota, for example, she had to surrender any property she owned to her husband. Similar laws left Pennsylvania women without rights to their property after a divorce. South Carolina forbade divorces altogether. This condemned many women to a lifetime with abusive or cheating husbands.

■ WORKING WOMEN

The growth of industry in the early 1900s meant that many women had more opportunities to work outside the home because factories were eager for workers. In 1900, 5.3 million American women were in the workforce. By 1910 that figure had jumped to 7.4 million. The greatest number of

WOMEN MAKE SHOES AT A FACTORY in New England around 1910.

An **AFRICAN AMERICAN LAUNDRESS** hangs sheets and stockings to dry. Women could earn money in their own homes by taking in other people's laundry.

a week. A small number of women found jobs as bookkeepers and cashiers, jobs previously reserved for men. Women from middle-class families trained as teachers or nurses.

Although many American women had jobs in the early 1900s, working outside the home was still relatively rare for females. Most women with jobs lived in homes without husbands or fathers who could work. Females who needed to earn a living for themselves challenged common wisdom that women must be sheltered, protected, and never let out alone. Many people worried that working left these women exposed to all sorts of tempting and immoral opportunities. Women with jobs onstage were thought especially prone to sexually loose living, so families tried to discourage their daughters from becoming singers, dancers, or actors.

women found jobs in service industries (industries such as hotels and banks that provide services instead of goods). Women ran boardinghouses, worked as salesclerks, or mended and sewed clothing. Recent immigrants or women of color often filled jobs as servants to wealthy white families. They washed clothes, cleaned homes, and cared for their employers' children.

Women who worked in factories were concentrated in the textile industry, an industry in which they outnumbered men. Textile industry workers wove cloth and made clothing. Days were long and wages low—sometimes only six to eight dollars

■ "WE STRIKE FOR JUSTICE"

The growing numbers of American working women jump-started the quest to establish better working conditions in U.S. industries. Women factory workers took the lead in calling for fairer work environments. They organized as far back as 1900 with a group that became the International Ladies Garment Workers' Union. Through strikes and public demonstrations, the factory workers changed the way that American women—and workers everywhere—battled unfair and unsafe treatment.

Working women took a giant leap into organizing in 1909. Growing anger against unjust work conditions reached a peak in two large New York clothing shops—Leiserson & Company and the Triangle Waist Company. Both refused to give their workers higher pay and shorter working hours. Workers at both shops struck, but bosses remained unmoved. Then the New York Women's Trade Union League called a meeting on November 22, 1909, to determine what to do next. Women from different shops spoke and debated about the best course of action. Tired of deliberating, a teenager named Clara Lemlich finally asked for the floor (the right to speak). She had participated in earlier strikes, in which police had attacked picket lines (lines of people standing together in protest) and

broken her ribs. Now she wanted action from everyone.

"I am tired of listening to speakers who talk in general terms . . . ," Lemlich announced. "What we are here for is to decide whether or not we shall strike. I offer a resolution that a general strike be declared—now!"

The crowd rallied around Lemlich, and the union called a strike. Women from throughout the industry walked out on their bosses the next morning, forming picket lines until their demands were met. Striking marchers carried banners that read, "We Strike for Justice."

The Women's Trade Union League expected three thousand workers to strike. But the strike hit a nerve. Tens of thousands of women formed picket lines. They braved freezing cold and hunger to gain a better work life. Workers and their cause caught the public's attention. More than one thousand new members joined the union each day of the strike. Wealthier women participated by aiding those in picket lines and paying for the bail

Tens of thousands of women formed picket lines. They braved freezing cold and hunger to gain a better work life.

WOMEN STRIKERS sell newspapers to support themselves during the Triangle Waist Company strike in New York in 1909.

(the temporary release of an imprisoned person in exchange for money) of those who got arrested. Reporters covered the story in newspapers.

The strike lasted until February 15, 1910. While many of the strikers' demands went unmet, the workers did make some important gains—such as the right to shorter working hours. Individual companies negotiated with their employees, and for the first time, women were seen as a major force behind organized labor.

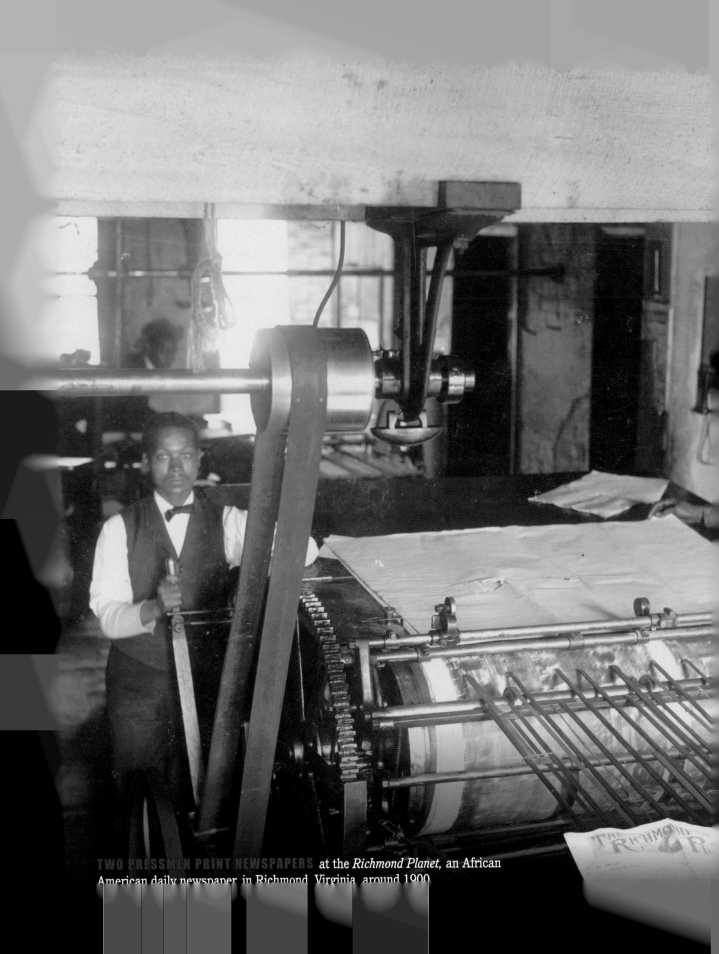

TWO PRESSMEN PRINT NEWSPAPERS at the *Richmond Planet*, an African American daily newspaper in Richmond, Virginia, around 1900.

Chapter Six

FROM MUCKRAKING TO FANTASY:
Writing of the 1900s

American literature and journalism of the early 1900s reflected the social climate of the time. Muckrakers investigated and wrote about corporate scandals and corruption. Magazines published exposés of unsafe work conditions. And many books explored the ideals of the decade. Novelists spun tales of gallant men and proper ladies.

New developments in printing allowed the written word to reach more readers, so books and articles of all kinds found wider audiences than they had in the past. Journalists and authors wrote for an expanding group of publishers, and printed works became an increasingly common form of entertainment.

■ NEWSPAPERS AND MAGAZINES

In the early 1900s, newspapers were the main source of news for most Americans. Nearly every medium-sized town had a morning and evening newspaper. Big cities sold competing papers. Twenty percent of newspapers published special Sunday editions. These included travel and entertainment sections, advertisements, and the latest form of reading amusement—comics. Popular comics characters included Buster Brown (a mischievous rich kid), Maud the Mule (a stubborn mare who often kicked her owner), and Little Jimmy (a forgetful boy who got into amusing scrapes).

Once editors discovered that sensational muckraking articles sold lots of magazines, magazines began to cover similar topics to those addressed in newspapers.

Previously, magazines such as *Atlantic, Harper's,* and *Scribner's* had published on a much smaller scale than newspapers. At thirty-five cents a copy, their reach extended to only about 130,000 readers. By 1900 magazines prices dropped to fifteen cents. Readership ballooned to 400,000 to 1 million readers. The content of magazines began to change too. Magazines originally published articles about people, places, and family life. But once editors discovered that sensational muckraking articles sold lots of magazines, magazines began to cover similar topics to those addressed in newspapers.

For example, journalist Ida Tarbell wrote a series of articles in *McClure's Magazine* titled "History of the Standard Oil Company." This exposé, published between 1902 and 1904, publicized the company's heavy-handed and destructive business practices. Muckracking journalist Lincoln Steffens also published notable articles in *McClure's.* His series called "Shame of the Cities" was a biting criticism of corrupt state and local governments. *Ladies' Home Journal* and *Collier's Weekly*—two very popular magazines of the era—exposed the hazards of unregulated medicines and false advertising.

Along with intriguing articles and more affordable prices, the advent of offset printing and photochemical processing contributed to magazines' success in the early 1900s. Before 1900 placing images in magazines was a long and painstaking process. It had to be done by hand, one image at a time. Printers Caspar Hermann and Ira Rubel experimented separately with ways to imprint photographic images onto aluminum plates coated with chemicals. Their experiments proved successful. The men began using the chemical-coated plates to make multiple images. They painted the plates with ink. Then they printed the inked image on a rubber pad and transferred—or offset—the image onto paper. The offset printing process allowed printers to produce short runs of magazines and brochures and eventually to add color. The addition of more photographs and the ability to add color allowed magazines and newspapers to easily create captions and slogans in their layouts.

 of the early 1900s most engaging investigative writers: Ida Tarbell.

Born in western Pennsylvania oil country in 1857, Tarbell became the only woman to graduate from Allegheny College in the class of 1880. She taught science for two years in Ohio before turning to writing. She used her inquiring scientific mind to doggedly pursue facts for articles.

During the 1890s, Tarbell wrote a successful series of articles about U.S. president Abraham Lincoln and French emperor Napoléon Bonaparte for the new monthly publication *McClure's Magazine.* But she soon turned her attention to an even bigger project: an exposé of the business practices behind John D. Rockefeller's Standard Oil Company. Tarbell had witnessed firsthand how large monopolies like Rockefeller's had changed the economic climate of her time. She'd seen how Standard Oil had harmed the businesses of independent oil workers—including that of her own father. These experiences prompted her decision to investigate the oil giant.

The result of Tarbell's investigations was her groundbreaking nineteen-part series titled "History of the Standard Oil Company" and published between 1902 and 1904. The detailed exposure of corruption led to

IDA TARBELL disliked the term *muckraker.* She considered herself a historian. Work like hers would later be called investigative journalism.

the U.S. government charging the company with violating the Sherman Anti-Trust Act. After years of trials, the courts finally broke up Standard Oil into smaller companies. Tarbell's landmark series opened the door to a landslide of muckraking articles and future reforms. Moreover, the articles defined investigative reporting.

Tarbell continued to write articles about government reform and key issues of the day in *American Magazine*, the journal she founded in 1906. Her work helped to transform ideas about women's roles in society. Tarbell was inducted into the National Women's Hall of Fame in 2000. Two years later, the U.S. Postal Service issued a stamp featuring her image.

By 1912 advances in photochemical processing led printers to be able to print up to eight thousand sheets per hour. These upgrades in technology revolutionized print production and permitted greater distribution of printed materials.

■ DIME NOVELS

During the late 1800s, publishers began to offer popular series fiction to American readers. Cheap booklets that cost ten cents each appeared in newsstands and dry goods stores. Dime novels, as these booklets were called, consisted of stories pitched to young, working-class readers. Early dime novels celebrated American ideals, with patriotic themes figuring heavily into the stories. Tales about the trials of backwoods settlers, complete with Native American battles, were also common. Orange papers served as covers, but no art appeared inside.

Into the 1900s, colored printing on covers and new story themes created enormous appeal for wider audiences. Themes expanded to include depictions of the Wild West and red-faced Native American villains (stereotyped images by modern standards), helpless women who needed to have their honor defended, romance, and sports heroes. Well-known dime-novel series included tales about Wild West characters Buffalo Bill and Jesse James. *Frank Leslie's Boys of America* told tales of adventure set in different historical periods.

The most popular series of stories was about a character named Frank Merriwell. Merriwell stories first appeared in *Tip Top Weekly* (an early 1900s magazine) and were later released as dime novels. Gilbert Patten, alias Burt L. Standish, wrote twenty thousand words a week about Merriwell. This perfect college man was smart, handsome, a top athlete, and an honorable person.

Story papers were an outgrowth of dime

This **DIME NOVEL** from the early 1900s features Dick Merriwell, Frank's younger brother.

novels. These eight-page weeklies offered similar stories to those found in dime novels—only they added art in the form of black-and-white wood engravings on the inside of the weeklies. Since story papers appealed to the entire family, they often attracted even greater numbers of readers than newspapers or magazines. Some issues sold four hundred thousand copies each.

■ 1900s LITERATURE

Dime novels and story papers weren't the only books that made an impact in the early 1900s. Titles that covered more serious topics also proved popular with American readers. One such book was *How the Other Half Lives*.

This volume, by muckraking author Jacob Riis, exposed the power of city bosses (unelected political leaders in urban communities) and how they conspired to keep the poor confined in neighborhoods with horrible living conditions. Riis was the first writer to take pictures to print with his works. His photos of urban squalor and decay shocked early-1900s readers.

Other authors penned stories of adventures and exciting locales. California native Jack London turned his adventurous life into enormously popular action-packed stories and novels. Although he had attended school only through the eighth grade, London continued his education by reading in public libraries and traveling around the country. Some of his most famous stories, *The Call of the Wild* (1903) and *White Fang* (1906), arose from his journeys to Alaska and the Yukon.

Author Kate Chopin found writing a release from the oppression she felt as a woman. Her works often examined problems in relationships

JACK LONDON'S *THE CALL OF THE WILD* is a story about a sled dog in the Yukon Territory. This illustration, by American artist Paul Bransom, appeared in a 1903 edition of London's book.

between men and women—a topic few American writers discussed in the early 1900s. Many of Chopin's writings aroused controversy. Her novel *The Awakening* (1899) proved the most controversial of all her works. This story exposed the hidden sexual passions of women and the heroine's desire for freedom from the constraints of marriage. The uproar spurred by the sexual content of *The Awakening* made it a frequent target for censorship in libraries. As a result, Chopin's publisher refused to publish her third collection of short stories. The scandal surrounding *The Awakening* lasted until Chopin's death in 1904. The book remained in a state of disgrace until it was revived as a result of the renewed interest in women's writing that came out of the women's movement of the 1960s. The novel was eventually made into a movie in 1994.

Some American authors questioned their world through characters in children's novels. To this day, young readers delight in L. Frank Baum's children's classic *The Wonderful Wizard of Oz* (1900). In this novel, heroine Dorothy finds an escape from her quiet life in Kansas when a cyclone carries her away to the Land of Oz. While in Oz, Dorothy meets fantastical characters who change her perspective on life in Kansas. Some readers have interpreted *The Wonderful Wizard of Oz* as a political allegory (a story that uses symbolism to make political statements). They claim that the characters Dorothy meets represent powerful eastern capitalists (the Wicked Witch of the East), naive farmers (the Scarecrow), soulless industrial workers (the Tin Woodman), and everyday American citizens (the Munchkins).

THE WONDERFUL WIZARD OF OZ was the first of L. Frank Baum's fourteen books about a strange and magical world.

Patrons study in the reading room of THE CARNEGIE LIBRARY OF HOMESTEAD, PENNSYLVANIA, around 1900. The library building included an athletic club.

One of the greatest contributions to early 1900s American literature came from steel magnate Andrew Carnegie. Originally from Scotland, Carnegie's family moved to the United States in the mid-1800s. Carnegie went on to make a fortune in the steel business. He sold his Carnegie Steel Company in 1901 and retired with a personal fortune of about $500 million. He then arranged to use some of his fortune to open public libraries across the United States. He said he wanted to provide people of modest means with greater access to books. As Carnegie explained, "I decided there was no use to which money could be applied so productive of good to boys and girls, who have good within them and ability and ambition to develop it, as the founding of a public library in a community. . . ."

Carnegie's donation funded 65 libraries in New York City. And the entrepreneur's charity didn't stop there. Over the next three decades, Carnegie gave $56 million to build 2,509 libraries in the English-speaking world. The United States was home to 1,679 of these, with at least one in every state except Rhode Island. Carnegie's donations led to the formation of the world's only network of free libraries.

Many communities were very proud of their new libraries. But not everyone who had worked for Carnegie found him charitable. Doubters believed that he had made his money off the sweat of the very people he professed to help. Indeed, as several of Carnegie's former employees noted, "We'd rather they hadn't cut our wages and let us spend the money for ourselves. What use has a man who works twelve hours a day for a library anyway?"

MARY CASSATT painted *The Swim, or Two Mothers and their Children on a Boat,* in 1910. Many of her paintings show moments in the lives of mothers and children.

Chapter Seven

IMPRESSIONISM TO GIBSON GIRLS:
1900s Arts, Architecture, and Fashion

In the early 1900s, the American art community tended to look toward Europe for trends and inspiration. As a result, U.S. artists, architects, and fashion designers often copied all things European. Impressionist paintings, grand Victorian homes, and British fashions caused the greatest stir. Even in this Euro-centered atmosphere, however, U.S. artists and designers managed to express themselves in unique ways.

◾ EUROPEAN INFLUENCES IN ART

Two artists in particular exemplify the impact Europeans had on American art. One was painter Mary Cassatt. Cassatt had originally studied painting at the Pennsylvania Academy of Fine Arts, but she soon found herself drawn to France. She traveled there to study in the 1860s. French impressionist painter Edgar Degas took an interest in Cassatt's work, so she stayed in France to learn more about Degas's style. She developed a style known for light colors and sketchy brushstrokes.

Lilla Cabot Perry was another painter heavily influenced by European techniques. Perry received her training at the Boston Cowles School in Massachusetts. Like Cassatt, she traveled to France to practice her art. While in France, Perry met the impressionist painter Claude Monet. He recognized Perry's talent and offered suggestions to help her fine-tune her methods. Unlike Cassatt, Perry eventually returned to the United States. She devoted her career to painting delicate portraits that showed the influence of her mentor, Monet.

■ COMIC STRIPS

Cassatt and Perry weren't the only ones making a splash in the early 1900s world of fine arts. Many Americans were attracted to a new and lighthearted form of art—comic strips. Researchers trace comic strips back to 1892. But the art form really took off with Richard Outcault's *The Yellow Kid* in 1896. *The Yellow Kid* ran in Joseph Pulitzer's newspaper the *New York World*. Pulitzer credited this strip with increasing his paper's circulation. The strip's popularity opened the door for several comic strips in the United States in the early 1900s.

By 1905 the elements of modern comic strips were set by such groundbreakers as Charles Edward (Bunny) Schultze's *Foxy Grandpa* (1900), James Swinnerton's *Little Jimmy* (1905), and the enormously popular *Buster Brown* (1902)—another Outcault creation. These weekly comic strips introduced readers to a regular set of characters, sequenced panels, and speech bubbles. *Buster Brown* became so famous that the strip influenced American dress and advertisements for decades. In 1907 *Mutt and Jeff* became the first well-known daily strip. Readers could follow the antics of their favorite characters every day rather than waiting an entire week for the story to continue.

Comic strip character **BUSTER BROWN** is a charming boy who gets into a lot of trouble. He keeps a talking dog, Tige, as a pet.

Many young American artists of the early 1900s debated whether to continue copying European styles or to develop art from the American experience. Several New York painters found their answer in classes they took with the free-spirited painting instructor Robert Henri. A native of Ohio, Henri urged his students to break with sentimental European art themes and paint realistic subjects from urban life. He recommended thick brushstrokes to reflect urban grit and energy.

In 1908 Henri and seven of his students held a groundbreaking exhibit in New York City, calling themselves the Eight. The show received mixed reviews. Some critics loved seeing familiar urban scenes in art, but others hated the subject matter. Hostile critics branded the Eight the Apostles of Ugliness or the Ashcan School. (The latter name derived from the fact that the artists painted the city as they saw it—complete with ash cans, or receptacles for holding trash.) These unfriendly labels actually freed the Eight from the restrictions typically placed on art of the era. The artists adopted the Ashcan label as their motto and continued to push their art and its subjects in new directions.

ROBERT HENRI painted *New York Winter* in 1902.

89

One of the best-known artists from the Ashcan School was George Bellows. Originally from Ohio, Bellows mainly painted urban scenes that showed people in action. Before he turned to painting, Bellows was an amateur baseball player, and his paintings often depicted sports scenes. He painted polo matches and prizefighting, with crowds of animated people cheering the athletes. Bellows became known for communicating energy and motion through his paintings.

1900s

AMERICA IN THE

Photography as an art form was just beginning to gain an audience in the 1900s. One man did more than any other to bring artful photography into the mainstream: Alfred Stieglitz. Stieglitz was born in Hoboken, New Jersey, in 1864. In the late 1800s, he became known for his pictorial photographs—soft-focus images with a hazy and romantic feel. In 1903 he began publishing the magazine *Camera Work*. This magazine featured the works of leading photographers and critics, and it helped to publicize the concept of photography as an art form.

Two years later, Stieglitz opened a New York City art gallery called 291. He displayed his own photography there as well as that of other artists. He also exhibited paintings and sculpture by modern European artists. Stieglitz was responsible for introducing millions of Americans to modern European painters such as Matisse, Cezanne, and Picasso.

Stieglitz married American painter Georgia O'Keeffe in 1924. She became a frequent subject of his photographs. Stieglitz took more

In 1907 ALFRED STIEGLITZ photographed immigrants returning to Europe by ship after being denied entry to the United States. He named this picture "The Steerage" after the crowded lower ship decks in which many immigrants traveled.

than three hundred photos of O'Keeffe—including some very famous, closely framed photos of her hands.

Stieglitz died in 1946. His pioneering work in artful photography left a lasting legacy in the United States and throughout the world.

■ KEWPIE CRAZE

Kewpie illustrations were another form of popular art. Kewpies were endearing, elflike characters created by Pennsylvania-born illustrator Cecilia Rose O'Neill. O'Neill was hired to adorn poems and stories in *Ladies' Home Journal* with her Kewpie characters.

Kewpies proved so popular that a comic strip about them emerged. The strip depicted Kewpies as warmhearted creatures who performed good deeds. O'Neill said the fanciful cupids were inspired by the baby brother she had cared for as a child. By 1909 Kewpies had touched so many readers that manufacturers reproduced them as paper cutouts and dolls. In one of the United States' first commercial crazes, buyers went wild for Kewpie likenesses on tableware, primary readers, and jewelry.

■ ARCHITECTURE

Some giant leaps in American architecture occurred at the turn of the century. At this time, Chicago was still rebuilding after a devastating fire that had destroyed the city in 1871, and many of the new buildings that sprang up were highly innovative. To prevent other disastrous fires, imaginative architects replaced wood dwellings with fireproof steel, glass, and reinforced concrete structures. Chicago architect Louis Sullivan and his contemporaries constructed tall buildings with steel beams for support—a new idea at the time. Such buildings paved the way for modern architecture of the future. Sullivan was particularly known for decorative steel patterns on the exteriors of his buildings.

The most famed architecture to emerge from the Chicago region was that of the Prairie School builders. *Prairie School* is a term used to describe the architectural style pioneered by former Sullivan employee and Oak Park, Illinois, native Frank Lloyd Wright. Wright rejected the ornate style of buildings that were popular in his day, and he hated the square brick or wood boxes where most families lived. Since Wright loved the American prairie and its simple beauty, he tried to incorporate aspects of nature into his creations.

> **" Form and function are one. "**
>
> —*architectural philosophy of Frank Lloyd Wright*
> *(1867–1959)*

Frank Lloyd Wright designed the **ARTHUR B. HEURTLEY HOUSE,** which was finished in 1902. Located in Oak Park, Illinois, the house is one of the earliest examples of Prairie School-style architecture.

Wright believed that buildings should fit into their surroundings. "Democracy needed something better than the box," he said. Following this thinking, Wright designed buildings low and wide, like the prairie. For materials, he used local stone, clay, and wood. He incorporated flower, grass, and leaf motifs into stained-glass windows and other building accents. When completed, his homes looked as if they belonged in their settings—whether they sat on a prairie, a mountainside, or in the woods. Wright said that "form and function are one" when it came to his buildings. By this he meant that the design of his buildings (their form) was well suited to their purpose (their function)—just as a bird's wings, a flower's petals, and other objects in nature are perfectly suited to their purposes. Wright was so influential that a number of American architects followed in his footsteps over the next twenty-five years, developing a uniquely American style of architecture that is still popular.

■ SEARS CATALOG HOMES

Wright influenced the nation's taste for simpler, more natural homes. But that didn't stop the retailer Sears, Roebuck and Co. from selling some very ornate houses through its mail-order Modern Homes program. This program allowed customers to choose from a variety of homes pictured in Sears's catalog and then order the materials necessary to build the home.

The Modern Homes program debuted in 1908. It took advantage of the boom in suburban home building that resulted from increased car travel. Sears's home designs ranged from a cozy cottage to a grand home with eleven rooms. Depending upon the size of the house, each plan cost between $695 and $4,115.

When a customer placed an order for a Sears home, two railroad boxcars carrying more than thirty thousand pieces of building materials arrived at the homeowner's nearest train depot. The homeowner also received a seventy-five-page instruction book explaining how to build the home. The most valuable information in the book was its disclaimer: "Do not take anyone's advice as to how this building should be assembled."

■ FASHION

American fashion gradually changed throughout the early 1900s, as ready-to-wear manufactured clothes replaced those made at home or by a tailor. Wealthy women could afford the latest in high fashion. Social norms demanded that they dress in fashions following trends from overseas—and especially from Britain.

Fashionable women and girls covered their bodies from head to toe, as was done in Britain. Hats with tall feathers or wide brims shaded the face. Lace fabric was wrapped around the neck to make it look long and slender. For most of the decade, fancier dresses were made in two pieces. Ankle-length, bell-shaped skirts flowed from the waist. They attached with dress fasteners to blouses decorated with ribbons, lace, embroidery, and beads. Gloves of kid, suede, or embroidered silk covered hands.

WEALTHY WOMEN show off the latest fashions at a garden party in Newport, Rhode Island, in 1905.

Working women often wore shirtwaist blouses. Shirtwaist blouses were tailored garments that looked like men's dress shirts. Women often tucked them into long skirts. Since most saleswomen, office workers, and teachers wore shirtwaists, demand for the blouses was high and many factories opened to manufacture them.

Beachwear for women required a scaled-down but nonetheless head-to-toe cover-up. To ensure that no part of the body was visible, girls wore loose-fitting pants, or pantaloons, underneath their bathing skirts. Only the brave dared to wear bloomers or knickers (loose-fitting short pants) as outerwear. Once bicycling spread as a popular sport for women, bloomers gained acceptance as sport dress. Still, many Americans opposed bloomer-wearing for any reason. They worried that women who wore men's clothing would embrace everything male, including a desire for women—and homosexuality was completely taboo at this time in American history.

According to the rules of fashion, women's bodies were supposed to look like the letter S—wider at the hips and chest and cinched tightly at the waist. The style was difficult and very uncomfortable to achieve. To obtain this shape, women fastened themselves into tight corsets that flattened their breasts and squeezed their waistlines. The corsets included hooks and eyes as fasteners in the back and vertical whalebones to maintain the stylish ladylike shape.

An American graphic artist named Charles Dana Gibson popularized the idea of the hourglass figure through his magazine illustrations. Gibson

Actress **CAMILLE CLIFFORD** embodied the S-curve ideal of the Gibson Girl look around 1900.

worked for *Life*, the most popular magazine in the country. In his weekly drawings for *Life*, he presented what he called "the American girl to all the world." This Gibson Girl, as she became known, was bold and daring. Gibson's pen-and-ink drawings depicted a woman with hair piled on top of her head, an unbelievably tiny waist, and the confidence to succeed in whatever Gibson pictured her doing. A sort of grown-up Barbie doll, she captured the imagination of the entire country.

American men of the 1900s followed fashion too. Their styles included three-button cutaway coats or single- or double-breasted jackets with straight lines. Pant legs measured a wide 22 inches (55 cm) at

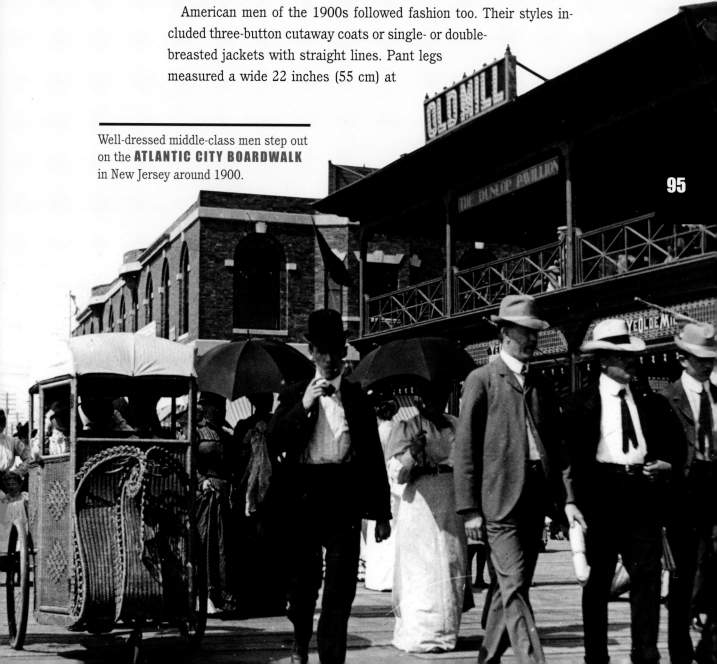

Well-dressed middle-class men step out on the **ATLANTIC CITY BOARDWALK** in New Jersey around 1900.

the bottom. A bow tie and high-top hat for special occasions completed the tailored look, along with short hair and a curled mustache. During work days, men often wore soft felt hats with rounded tops. These were called derby hats. Summer attire sometimes included a straw boater hat with a flat top encircled with a ribbon. Wool or felt hats with a creased top kept men warm in winter.

Three-piece suits were enormously popular for men. Even men of modest means often owned at least one three-piece suit. These suits were usually made of a dark-colored twill material. Later in the decade, more casual tweed jackets appeared. These became popular among men with office jobs.

Males of high social status often owned separate wardrobes for evening outings. These included knee-length overcoats and walking sticks with silver handles. Underneath the overcoats, men donned dark pants and coats with tails. Dress shirts sported winged or shawl collars or satin or silk trim. A gold pocket watch, fine leather gloves, and a high silk hat were popular eveningwear accessories.

Men's beachwear was modest—much like bathing attire for women. Men were not expected to cover up from head to toe, but they did typically cover their chests with long, short-sleeved knit bathing shirts. They paired the bathing shirts with long shorts that extended halfway to the knees.

THREE SWIMMERS WADE INTO THE OCEAN around 1905. Both men and women covered up for swimming.

THREE CHILDREN HAVE A TEA PARTY AROUND 1900. The older girl wears a miniature version of an adult's dress, and the boy wears a three-piece suit with short pants. Very young children of both sexes often wore plain dresses like the one worn by the child in the center.

One fashion craze that caught on with both men and women was the desire for tiny-looking feet. Tiny feet were a sign of high fashion in the early 1900s. People often squeezed into ill-fitting shoes to make their feet look smaller. Some women even had their baby toes removed to squeeze into slenderer shoes!

■ CHILDREN'S CLOTHING

For the most part, American parents dressed their children like miniature adults. Girls between the ages of one and five wore short dresses. Young boys often dressed up in three-piece suits that included vests. These suits featured knee-length pants rather than long trousers. Boys wore long stockings that met the pants at the knee.

Sailor suits were the one fashion that was just for kids. Girls wore navy blue sailor dresses with wide waists and large white collars, and boys dressed in two-piece navy blue suits with knee pants. Sailor suits for children remained popular on and off for decades.

BERT WILLIAMS *(RIGHT)* AND GEORGE WALKER *(CENTER)* perform in a variety show around 1905. Walker's wife, Aida Overton Walker *(left)*, a dancer and choreographer, also appeared in the show. In this picture, George Walker wears what is known as "blackface," theatrical makeup that emphasizes racist stereotypes of African American appearance.

Chapter Eight

THE THRILL OF ENTERTAINMENT:
Theater and Movies in the 1900s

Stage and screen entertainment flourished in the United States during the early 1900s. From minstrel shows to Broadway plays, live theater attracted legions of fans. The budding movie industry also drew large audiences. Film and theater buffs flocked to see all the shows the decade had to offer.

■ MINSTREL SHOWS

Minstrel shows began in the 1830s and remained popular across the country into the twentieth century. During these live performances, white performers blackened their faces with burned cork or greasepaint and played the role of African Americans. The main reason for the charade was to mock African Americans for white audiences. Entertainers sang, danced, and presented skits that depicted negative stereotypes of blacks, such as the Jim Crow character.

By the beginning of the twentieth century, African American men began to perform as part of the minstrel act. Minstrel shows were one of the few opportunities open to African Americans who wanted to perform onstage. Famous African American minstrels, such as Bert Williams and his performing partner, George Walker, got their start playing the African American men they actually were. Williams and Walker went on to pioneer successful African American shows written and presented by African Americans. They presented these shows to both African American and Caucasian audiences. While the shows included many of the same unflattering black characters from earlier minstrel acts, they helped introduce white Americans to the lively beat of ragtime tunes and the coming Jazz Age. Versions of minstrel shows continued into the 1950s, until the growing civil rights movement put an end to these racist depictions of African American inferiority.

■ VAUDEVILLE

Vaudeville was a popular outgrowth of minstrel shows during the early twentieth century. A vaudeville show was a series of unrelated acts on-stage, one after another—much like minstrel shows. Vaudeville shows usually traveled in circuits. For example, an act might tour different states in the East Coast. The first vaudeville programs from the late 1890s included everything from singers, dancers, and comedians to dog and bicycle acts and magicians.

In 1900 champion bicycle racer Marshall "Major" Taylor challenged fellow cyclist Charlie "Mile-a-Minute" Murphy onstage as part of their performance with the Keith Vaudeville Company in Massachusetts. The Keith Company

"I am confident that the maximum speed on the bicycle has not been reached."

—bicycle racer Marshall "Major" Taylor (1878–1932)

was the biggest vaudeville company in the East. The two athletes rode their bicycles on a stage, balancing them on home trainers (stationary machines with rollers). Audiences followed their progress in 5-mile (8 km) heats by watching large arrows connected to counters on the bikes. Fans delighted in the stationary competition.

One theatrical producer, George Lederer, wrote sketches that linked different vaudeville acts into one story. Lederer staged elaborate sets and outfitted performers in eye-catching costumes. He added beautiful women who were scantily clad by the era's standards, defying strict views of female etiquette. The shows made a big splash in New York City in the early 1900s.

By the end of the decade, every town boasted at least one theater for local and traveling vaudeville acts. These acts often provided the training ground for plays and musicals that eventually became successful on Broadway, a wide avenue in New York City.

lorenz Ziegfeld Jr. was a well-known American vaudeville producer. Born in Chicago, Illinois, in 1869, he made a name for himself by putting on remarkable Broadway productions from the early 1900s to the 1920s. Ziegfeld's best-known vaudeville acts featured songs, dances, and comedy sketches as well as a chorus line of beautiful women. The women flaunted their figures onstage and shocked audiences with their revealing costumes.

While Ziegfeld's chorus lines portrayed women as sex objects, the famed producer was quite progressive when it came to race. He became one of the first producers to hire an African American performer when he invited Bert Williams to join his show, and Ziegfeld was a fierce defender of civil rights. He called the bluff of some of his performers who claimed that they would quit if Williams joined the act. Ziegfeld even threatened to move out of his apartment building when his doorman refused to allow Williams up for dinner.

Ziegfeld had a keen eye for talent, and he launched the careers of many future stars.

FLORENZ ZIEGFELD JR. is most famous for the *Ziegfeld Follies*, a series of Broadway variety shows. The first show opened in 1907.

Motion-picture actresses Marion Davies and Irene Dunne got their start in Ziegfeld productions. Ziegfeld also helped to promote Will Rogers and Fanny Brice—two popular entertainers and comedians.

Ziegfeld died in 1932. While vaudeville shows like his eventually fell out of favor, the shows he created influence Broadway entertainment to this day.

101

■ BROADWAY THEATER

In 1900 thirty-three theaters lined Broadway. More opened at a rapid rate, to meet demand. The theaters were beautiful and very elegant. Their architecture mirrored grand European opera houses. Theater-goers sat on plush velvet seats in rooms illuminated with the latest gaslights. In 1903 the first electric theater marquee appeared on Times Square, a major New York City intersection. This new invention from Thomas Edison heralded the gala performance inside. Soon so many of the city's theaters advertised with brightly lit marquees that Broadway earned the nickname the Great White Way. By 1908 theater tickets began selling for $2.50—about $50 in modern-day currency and considered very expensive at the time. Broadway theater was entertainment for the top-hat-and-fur-coat crowd.

All forms of entertainment appeared on Broadway. One particularly successful show came about in 1905 when British novelist J. M. Barrie turned one of his stories into a play. The story portrayed Peter Pan, a boy who could fly and who never grew up. Actress Maude Adams acted the part of Peter Pan for eight years on Broadway.

 OTHER CROWD-PLEASERS ONSTAGE

Two other types of performances reached their peak in the United States during the early 1900s. One was magic shows. Harry Houdini put on the most popular magic shows of his

This poster advertised **MAUDE ADAMS AS PETER PAN** in J. M. Barrie's 1905 play.

day. Born Erik Weisz in 1874 to German and Hungarian immigrant parents, Houdini and his family emigrated from Hungary to the United States in the 1870s.

Houdini lost his father at an early age. To earn money to help support his mother, he turned his physical stamina and winning personality into a vaudeville act. Houdini had studied the magic techniques of French magician Jean-Eugène Houdin and later changed his name to Houdini to honor the magician. (The name Harry came from a nickname Houdini had in childhood.) Houdini soon won fame in the United States by performing daring feats as an escape artist.

In 1900 Houdini toured Europe as the King of Handcuffs, a name he got from his ability to easily work his way out of handcuffs. By the time he returned to the United States, his image was set. Throughout the first two decades of the 1900s, Houdini gradually attempted more difficult escapes that tested his body and mind. He disappeared from tight spots of all kinds. He broke out of a jail cell. He wriggled out of straitjackets while suspended upside down in water tanks. Each new escape earned him more publicity, and he eventually became world famous. Houdini's popularity continued until his death on October 31, 1926. By then he was called the Genius of Escape.

The other wildly popular show that captured the American public's imagination was Buffalo Bill's Wild West show—a jumble of acts that promoted the myth of cowboys and Indians of the American West. In the 1880s, William Cody, known as Buffalo Bill, turned his experiences as a buffalo hunter and army scout into a colorful show. Audiences in

HARRY HOUDINI, billed as the King of Handcuffs, posed for this portrait around 1905 with his hands and feet chained.

the East and around the world thrilled to trick riders, ropers, shooters, wild animals, and about one hundred Native Americans reenacting war dances and attacks on stagecoaches.

Cody and the popularity of his shows cemented forever the world's image of the American West. Although Cody always treated Native Americans with respect, his show's pretend battles helped ingrain the idea that Native Americans were savage. Other acts featured vaqueros, or Mexican cowboys, and buffalo hunts—both long gone from the frontier by then.

Cody's show went on a final European tour in 1903. The company returned to the United States to great acclaim. By 1907, however, the Wild West show faced money problems. For the next three years, Cody took the show on a series of final cross-country tours, but finances never improved. The glory days of the show were over. Still, the image of the Wild West of Native Americans, rough riders, and bronco busters lived on in books and movies glorifying the American Wild West.

This poster advertises **BUFFALO BILL'S WILD WEST SHOW**. The show featured horseback riding stunts and mock battles between cowboys and Native Americans.

One of the most celebrated acts in Buffalo Bill's Wild West show involved Annie Oakley. Born Phoebe Ann Moses in 1860, Oakley grew up in a poor and loving family in western Ohio. After her father died when she was five, her family struggled to survive. Oakley was known to shoot squirrels for food. By the age of fifteen, Oakley was shooting game to sell. She paid off her mother's mortgage. And she won fifty dollars in a shooting contest against the famous marksman Frank Butler, who took a liking to Oakley.

The two sharpshooters married and toured as a shooting act. They joined circuses and vaudeville shows. After William Cody saw Oakley shoot, he hired her and Butler for his Wild West show in 1885. By then Oakley had dropped her birth name in favor of her stage name: Annie Oakley. She became a major star in Cody's act.

Oakley was fast, cocky with a gun, and accurate. She twirled her pistol. She shot playing cards or cigarette butts out of her husband's lips at thirty paces. Oakley captured the imagination of everyone who believed that gun-toting meant survival in the West—even for women.

Oakley stayed with the Wild West show for sixteen years, crisscrossing the country to perform. Cody's show made Oakley a household name and launched her career in stage productions. In 1902 she starred

ANNIE OAKLEY poses with her rifle and shooting awards around the turn of the century. She continued to set shooting records until she was more than sixty years old.

in a stage play called *The Western Girl.* She played a straight-shooting heroine. Other shows followed.

In 1915 Oakley began giving women shooting lessons. She also put on shows for charity. By the time Oakley died in 1926, she had become a role model for many girls and women. A 1946 Broadway musical called *Annie Get Your Gun* told a fictionalized version of Oakley's life story.

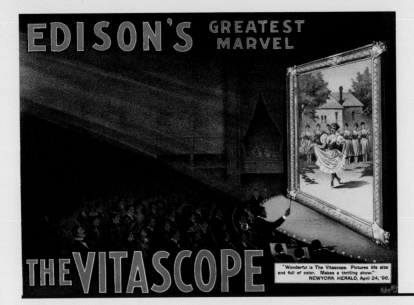

An ad for Thomas Edison's **VITASCOPE** shows moviegoers watching a film while an orchestra provides the soundtrack. By 1904, movies with fictional stories and famous actors were the most popular with viewers.

■ MOVING PICTURES: PEEP SHOWS AND NICKELODEONS

When Thomas Edison first developed the motion-picture camera in 1888, he wanted his invention to make money. But it took another six years before he devised a way for people to see motion pictures. Edison encased the moving camera in 50 feet (15 m) of looped film on a reel in a box. For a penny, individual viewers watched the film action through a tiny hole in the box. Peep-show machines, as these contraptions were called, displayed dancing women, romping dogs, acrobats, speeding trains, and other scenes.

The concept caught on. Americans loved seeing still pictures explode with movement, and Edison was pleased to earn money from his idea.

In 1896 Edison patented another projector called the vitascope, invented by his employee Thomas Armat. This machine projected moving pictures onto a large screen so that many people could watch at once. Soon makeshift theaters began using the vitascope to show movies. The first films lasted between ten and twelve minutes. They cost a couple hundred dollars to make and could be filmed in one day.

Once other companies learned about the technology, they tried to compete. Edison hired lawyers to fend off rivals who copied his inventions. Meanwhile, his company worked to keep ahead of his competitors. Edison's company made one of the first storytelling motion pictures in 1903. The 11.2-minute *Great Train Robbery* was a silent Western shot

> **" It will do for the eye what the phonograph does for the ear. "**
>
> —*inventor Thomas Edison (1847–1931), describing motion-picture technology*

THE GREAT TRAIN ROBBERY was a Western film made in 1903. It used new techniques in filmmaking, and some scenes were hand tinted to appear in color.

in New Jersey. It showed two bandits who tried to rob a train depot agent. The movie was an instant hit. Audiences became so engaged in the film that they shouted, "Catch 'em!" as the bandits ran away. The movie went on to earn two million dollars in profits in five years—a large sum for the time.

Movie houses in converted storefronts and barns sprang up across the nation. These early movie theaters were called nickelodeons. The name combined the word *nickel,* a reference to the five-cent price of admission, with the Greek word *odeon,* which means

"theater." Nickelodeons presented shows that were between fifteen and ninety minutes long. The nickel entry fee was cheap enough that Americans earning even the smallest of salaries could afford a movie break now and then. Non-English-speaking immigrants especially liked the fact that the films had no sound and language comprehension was not an issue. Instead, piano players accompanied the action on the screen with fast, slow, lively, or grim tunes depending on the mood of each scene. A new era of entertainment was beginning.

AFRICAN AMERICAN CHILDREN SING as one boy plays the piano around 1910. Many people learned to play popular songs for themselves and their friends in the early 1900s.

Chapter Nine

MOVING TO MUSICALS AND RAGTIME:
Music and Dance in the 1900s

Most American music of the early 1900s mirrored happenings around the country. Some popular songs—such as "Come Josephine in My Flying Machine" and "In My Merry Oldsmobile"—highlighted the latest in transportation inventions. Others—including "The Preacher and the Bear"—spotlighted the problem of racism.

Barbershop quartets were popular and were known for their amazing ability to harmonize. African Americans organized the first barbershop quartets in black neighborhoods, where men who wanted to sing harmony formed impromptu groups in barbershops and alleyways. Then phonographs were invented, and performers were needed to record music. That's when white singers began organizing their own barbershop quartets. They gathered in recording studios to capture their harmonies on records. The records were a big hit with early-1900s music fans.

■ MUSICALS

Broadway musicals gave Americans another popular form of music: show tunes. Among the most beloved show tunes of the era came from George M. Cohan, an Irish American native of Rhode Island. Critics sometimes complained that Cohan's songs sounded too simplistic. But audiences loved them. They often left theaters humming patriotic tunes such as "The Yankee Doodle Boy" (from the 1904 musical *Little Johnny Jones*) and "You're a Grand Old Flag" (from the 1906 show *George Washington, Jr.*).

Broadway composer Victor Herbert wrote more sophisticated songs than Cohan. Herbert's operettas and musical comedies required classically trained voices that could produce a range of melodies. Like Cohan, Herbert often wrote about patriotic themes—but his songs favored everyday issues over military and government cheerleading. Through the years, many of Herbert's best-known musicals—such as *Babes in Toyland* (1903) and *Naughty Marietta* (1910)—have continued to find new audiences.

■ RAGTIME

Another early-1900s musical sensation was Scott Joplin. This African American composer from Texas pioneered the style of music known as ragtime. Ragtime combines syncopated melodies (a musical accent that stresses the weak beat, creating a lively rhythm) with regularly accented accompaniments.

Lively ragtime tunes were typically played on the piano. They first became popular in the southern and midwestern United States, where ragtime pianists played their compositions before eager audiences. Missouri in particular became a cultural center for ragtime musicians and their fans. The state's many saloons provided welcoming venues for traveling ragtime stars.

By the early 1900s, ragtime music seemed to be everywhere. Young people, black and white, embraced its syncopated rhythms, unique beat, and free, spontaneous sound. But not everyone approved of the ragtime trend. Some parents feared that ragtime music would corrupt their children's morals. Its loose, irregular beat and diverse rhythms threatened those not used to the

❝Got more trouble than I can stand, Ever since ragtime has struck the land— Never saw the like in all my days; Ev'ryone has got the ragtime craze.❞

—from "I'm Certainly Living a Rag-Time Life," a ragtime song written by Gene Jefferson and Robert S. Roberts in 1900

cott Joplin was born in Texas around 1868. He left home as a teen and settled in Missouri around 1894. A self-taught pianist and cornet player, Joplin first played his edgy style of music on upright pianos in Missouri's saloons and honky-tonk establishments.

Joplin often played piano in the Maple Leaf Club, a Sedalia, Missouri, saloon. When a Sedalia music store owner agreed to publish Joplin's first piece of music in 1899, Joplin named the piece the "Maple Leaf Rag." In the first year it was published, only about four hundred sheet-music copies of the "Maple Leaf Rag" sold. Within a decade, however, half a million copies had sold—including thousands through the popular national chain store F. W. Woolworth.

In 1901 Joplin moved to Saint Louis, Missouri, where many ragtime pioneers worked. He wanted to devote more time to composing. While there, he wrote such favorites as "Sunflower Slow Drag" and "Peacherine Rag." The "Strenuous Rag," another popular tune, was Joplin's tribute to Theodore Roosevelt and his famous meeting with Booker T. Washington.

SCOTT JOPLIN wrote some of the most famous songs of the 1900s, including "The Entertainer" and "The Maple Leaf Rag."

Throughout the 1900s, Joplin wrote other ragtime songs, and he also penned some operas. Yet he never achieved fame and fortune as a composer during his lifetime. In 1973 the movie *The Sting* featured his music—including his well-known hit "The Entertainer"—and its film score won an Academy Award. The revival of Joplin's work helped to spur awareness of ragtime and its status as one of the first truly American forms of music.

style. The music world also questioned the validity of ragtime. A 1900 edition of the *Etude,* a publication for musicians, called ragtime's rhythms "double-jointed jumping jack airs that fairly twist the ears of an educated musician from their anchorage."

a Rainey helped give birth to blues music as one of its first singing and recording stars. Born Gertrude Pridgett in 1886 in Columbus, Georgia, Rainey sang from her earliest days. At fourteen she sang in a talent show and soon began traveling with vaudeville troupes. While touring she met minstrel show manager William "Pa" Rainey, and the two of them married in 1904. Rainey changed her name to Ma Rainey, and she toured with her husband as part of the F. S. Wolcott's Rabbit Foot Minstrels.

Rainey toured with her husband for about three decades, performing throughout the United States and in Mexico. Eventually, Rainey's marriage broke up, and in 1923, she began making records with the recording company Paramount. Between 1923 and 1928, Rainey recorded one hundred of her signature blues songs with some of the greatest musicians of the time, including Louis Armstrong and Tommy Dorsey. Her "See See Rider Blues" and "Jelly Bean Blues" became classics.

Rainey's recording days ended in 1928, and she returned to Columbus. She owned

MA RAINEY poses in a 1923 promotional photo for one of her solo records.

and ran two theaters before dying in 1939. But her blues legacy lived on, influencing such singers and songwriters as Francis Cabrel and Bob Dylan. In 1982 playwright August Wilson wrote *Ma Rainey's Black Bottom* to honor the song Rainey wrote of the same name. The U.S. Postal Service created a stamp in her honor in 1994, and "See See Rider Blues" became part of the Grammy Hall of Fame as well as the Library of Congress National Recording Registry in 2004.

In spite of its detractors, ragtime thrived throughout the 1900s. This musical style holds an important place in musical history, and it paved the way for a later form of popular music—jazz.

■ BRASS BANDS

While many music fans in the early 1900s were jiving to ragtime favorites, others were enjoying very different sorts of tunes: brass-band marching compositions. Brass-band music had been around since the nation's earliest history. But rousing marching songs really began to take off around the time of the Civil War in the mid-1800s. The popularity of such songs lasted well into the early twentieth century.

Marching songs typically have patriotic themes. They appealed to Americans' sense of pride in their country, much like Cohan's American-themed show tunes. Marching songs were a cultural institution in the early 1900s. They frequently took center stage at social events ranging from parades and holiday gatherings to state fairs and summer band shell concerts.

The most popular marching-band leader of the 1900s was John Philip Sousa. Born in Washington, D.C., Sousa served as conductor of the U.S. Marine Band for twelve years in the late 1800s before obtaining a discharge

JOHN PHILIP SOUSA AND HIS BAND played at New York's Empire Theatre in 1910.

from the marines and forming a band of his own. Sousa's Band, as Sousa and his musicians were known, made a number of popular phonograph recordings and toured the country extensively. Fans of marching-band music flocked to hear Sousa hits such as "Hail to the Spirit of Liberty" and "Stars and Stripes Forever." To this day, Sousa's songs define the spirit of patriotism, and they are often heard at Independence Day celebrations around the country.

■ DANCING TO THE MUSIC

Before the twentieth century, the only dances most Americans knew were those that came from Europe. These included the waltz, the polka, and the schottische. But with the introduction of ragtime and other new musical styles, Americans were ready to usher in new forms of dance.

The dances that people embraced throughout the ragtime era were highly expressive and individualistic—much like ragtime music itself. No formal

Dancers demonstrate the solo and couples' versions of **THE CAKEWALK** in the early 1900s.

Many ragtime-era dances seemed too immodest to conservative Americans. This cartoon from the early 1900s, titled "**TURKEY TROT,**" shows real animals looking scandalized by people performing the dance.

training was required to learn them. One early ragtime-era dance was called the cakewalk. This dance had ragtime fans strutting and high stepping in time to the music. Another was known as the turkey trot. Dancers performed this step to the "Maple Leaf Rag" and other upbeat tunes. The dance consisted of a springy, hopping walk with feet placed far apart. Many found the turkey trot risqué and sexually suggestive. It caused an uproar among the upper classes and conservative Americans.

The turkey trot was just one in a string of dances named for animals. Other "animal dances" included the bunny hug, the grizzly bear, and the camel walk. All the animal dances got dancers swaying, swinging, and shaking to ragtime's syncopated beat—and all caused polite society to raise its eyebrows. Many of the ragtime dances traced their roots to African American dance traditions. Racist attitudes of the era—coupled with concerns about dance steps that some deemed inappropriate because of their easy physicality—kept much of mainstream white America from accepting ragtime dance trends.

"Nobody has ever done that."

—Annie Edson Taylor, explaining why she chose to plunge over Niagara Falls in a barrel in 1901

Watchers help **ANNIE EDSON TAYLOR** *(right)* to shore after her daring 1901 trip over Niagara Falls *(above)*.

Chapter Ten

DARING **AND SPEED:**

Sports and Recreation in the 1900s

On October 24, 1901, Annie Edson Taylor squeezed into a 4.5-foot-high (1.3 m) and 3-foot-wide (1 m) barrel. The Michigan school-teacher strapped herself inside the oiled oak container and placed a pillow behind her head. Workers from the beer-cask company that had built the airtight barrel bolted it shut and forced air inside with a bicycle pump. At 4:05 P.M., the barrel was released into the rushing waters leading to New York's raging Niagara Falls. Taylor plunged 170 feet (52 m) over the falls into the thick haze below.

Many men had tried the same stunt before her. Taylor, however, was the first person—man or woman—to survive. "Nobody has ever done that," was Taylor's response when reporters asked her why she'd attempted the daring feat.

Taylor represented the sporting spirit of the early 1900s. Americans of the era liked their sports rough-and-tumble. Not all athletes were daredevils like Taylor. But most tried to push the limits of speed and endurance in team and individual sports.

■ BASEBALL

By the early twentieth century, baseball was the United States' most popular team sport. Boys and men swatted balls in empty city lots and farm fields. Most sizable towns hosted their own amateur baseball teams. In 1900 eight cities organized their teams into the professional American League, a rival to the twenty-four-year-old National League. Neither team allowed African Americans or women to compete. Still, with these leagues, fans had two professional baseball leagues and twice as many games to cheer. They were thrilled. At their first game in Chicago, American-League players "were almost swamped with unexpected popularity. . . ," according to an April 23, 1900, article in the *Chicago Daily Tribune.* "There were not enough tickets to go around and not enough seats."

THE CHICAGO WHITE STOCKINGS won the 1900 American League pennant.

At first, competition between the two leagues was stiff. The National League claimed the new American League players were stealing their fans. After three years of wrangling, the rivals agreed to join forces. They concurred that their games would follow the same set of rules, and at the end of every season, the top team from each league would compete in a playoff to decide the world champion.

On October 1, 1903, the American League champions, the Boston Pilgrims, played the National League's winning Pittsburgh Pirates in Boston. The two teams were to battle each other for nine games, or until one team clearly won the most games in the nation's first World Series. The series ended after eight games, with Boston winning five to three. The *Pittsburgh Press* reported overflow crowds.

Boston's Denton True "Cy" Young became the American League's first star. His pitching won two of the first World Series games. During his career, he won 511 games—about 100 more than any other pitcher in history. In 1904 his hitless streak ran twenty-four innings, only to be broken by another future Hall of Famer Sam Crawford.

To celebrate the country's love of baseball, vaudeville entertainer Jack Norworth wrote the song "Take Me Out to the Ball Game" in 1908. The hit emerged as the nation's baseball anthem. Fans sing Norworth's cheery tune at ball games to this day.

Although many Americans thought sports to be unfeminine, women loved playing baseball too. Women in ankle-length skirts and team blouses batted balls and ran bases. The first wave of athletes came from women's colleges and then coeducational institutions. Even in coed schools, coaches kept men and women separate.

In 1904 five female students at the University of Pennsylvania dared to

Record-breaking pitcher **CY YOUNG** warms up at a 1909 game.

THE STAR BLOOMER GIRLS BASEBALL CLUB played in Indianapolis, Indiana, during the early 1900s.

omen throughout the United States joined baseball teams in the early 1900s. One well-known female team was called the Bloomer Girls. They were named after Amelia Jenks Bloomer, an American supporter of women's rights who designed the loose-fitting pants worn by most of the players. The Bloomer Girls achieved fame by traveling the country and challenging men's amateur and semiprofessional teams.

Many of the Bloomer Girls' players were enormously talented. They played hard—and they usually won. The Bloomer Girls were so respected that men of-ten joined their team. The men wanted to practice and hone their playing skills so that they might break into professional baseball. Teenage boys and men gladly dressed in bloomers for the chance to pitch and catch with gifted Bloomer Girls teammates. Hall of Famers Roger Hornsby and Joe Wood started their careers as Bloomers. They were called toppers after the wavy-haired wigs they wore to pass for women.

The Bloomer Girls never got to play with the pros or attend the World Series. But they broke many gender barriers and paved the way for women athletes of the future.

join the men's baseball team. Crowds applauded the runners, who were slowed by their flowing and often ripping skirts. When university officials heard about the coed teams, however, they banned women from playing baseball anywhere on school grounds. From then on, protests against women playing baseball increased, even at all-girls' schools. One by one, colleges abolished their women's baseball teams. By then, enthusiasm for women's baseball had spread beyond colleges and universities to neighborhood lots and playgrounds.

FOOTBALL

The United States had many professional football teams in the 1900s. But an even bigger sensation was the college football league. College teams played about eleven games in a fall season, and every major newspaper covered the events. Fans went crazy watching football players and their often-aggressive behavior as the game spread to more universities and high schools throughout the nation.

In 1902 colleges began the tradition of sending the best teams to end-of-the-season bowl games. Pasadena, California, hosted Stanford University and the University of Michigan for what became the first New Year's Day Rose Bowl game. From then on, football grew into a moneymaking business. Some big-name college games brought in almost forty thousand dollars each.

Educators hotly debated the value of encouraging team sports. They feared that education was beginning to take a backseat to athletics. School

officials also questioned the lack of protective gear for players. The first football-related death in 1900 inflamed the controversy. A runner from Lake Forest College in Illinois died after other players tackled and accidentally smothered him during a game. Arguments against school football peaked in 1905. That season, nineteen high school and college players died.

President Roosevelt finally intervened. He ordered representatives from sixty-two colleges to meet and come up with a plan to control the aggressiveness in football. The group formed the National Collegiate Athletic Association (NCAA), an organization that pioneered new rules for college football. In 1910 the NCAA banned players from locking arms as they ran down the field. They forbade the flying wedge—a dangerous move in which ten players assembled in a V formation and plowed into the defense. To further protect players, the NCAA ordered them to wear the first protective gear—a leather helmet.

BASKETBALL

Basketball was an instant success from the time it first began. In 1891 James Naismith had wanted to perk up his physical education class at the

Educators hotly debated the value of encouraging team sports. They feared that education was beginning to take a backseat to athletics.

JAMES NAISMITH, inventor of basketball, stands with a ball and a peach basket on a college playing field. Players shot at baskets with closed bottoms until 1906, when they were replaced with metal hoops.

Massachusetts Young Men's Christian Association (YMCA) Training School. He created thirteen rules for two teams made up of nine players to run, dribble, and shoot a mushy ball into a raised peach basket. The game took off at East Coast colleges, both male and female. By the turn of the century, men were earning money playing in professional basketball leagues. The players were often called cagers after the wire cages that surrounded basketball courts to prevent wild balls from flying into the balcony. In 1904 men's basketball became a part of the Olympics, spreading the sport to other countries.

Despite some people's claim that basketball was unladylike, physical education teacher Clara Gregory Baer introduced the sport to her female students at Sophie Newcomb College in New Orleans, Louisiana. Teachers there worried that two-handed throws forced shoulders forward, causing "a consequent flattening of the chest." To escape flat chests, women at Newcomb used a one-hand setup shot.

The women at Sophie Newcomb also wore special uniforms. The outfits were a far cry from the sleeveless shirts and short pants that male basketball players wore. Instead, the women's uniforms consisted of corsets covered with full, divided skirts and high-necked, long-sleeved blouses. High, dark stockings inside soft, slipperlike shoes covered the legs. After each game, the players' hairpins and delicate linen handkerchiefs littered the gym floor.

■ SOCCER

Soccer, which the world outside the United States calls football, had a limited audience among U.S. sports fans—although Native Americans had been playing a version of the game for years. During the early 1900s, waves of immigrants arrived from European countries where soccer was popular. They organized clubs and teams to play, sparking some interest in soccer.

In 1904 a men's U.S. soccer team formed to play in the Olympics. But even with its worldwide appeal, soccer remained a difficult sell in the United States.

■ INDIVIDUAL ATHLETIC ABILITY

As opportunities for leisure increased, many Americans sought individual athletic activities to fill their time. They took part in events that showcased speed, strength, and toughness. Tennis and swimming became favorite sports of wealthy families. These activities drew people as both spectators and participants.

Tennis, in particular, attracted many fans in the early 1900s. In 1900 Harvard University tennis star Dwight Davis was so inspired by the nation's enthusiasm for his sport that he contributed a trophy to promote international competition. Three men from Great Britain agreed to play the first match against Davis and his all-Harvard team for the trophy. The British players lost, but a new tradition of a yearly Davis Cup tournament began.

Women's tennis found stars as well. University of California student Hazel Hotchkiss Wightman commanded the court from her earliest tennis days. In 1909 she earned her first of four wins in the U.S. Women's Championship games.

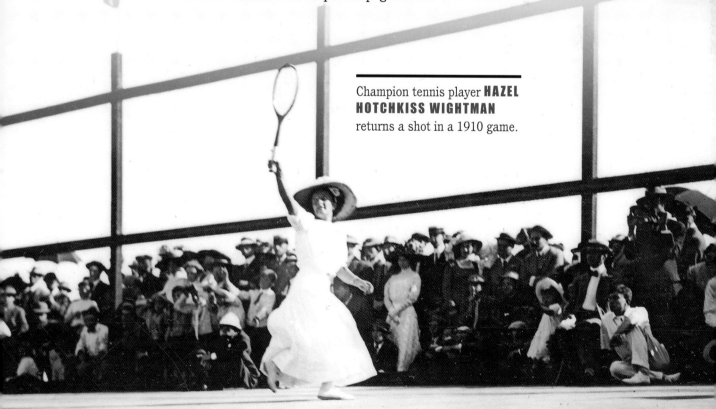

Champion tennis player **HAZEL HOTCHKISS WIGHTMAN** returns a shot in a 1910 game.

Wightman continued to dominate the sport throughout the early 1900s, earning forty-four national titles in all.

One of the most exciting sports at the turn of the century was boxing. Boxing provided the opportunity for athletes of any economic class to compete. Recent immigrants, poor folks, and African Americans punched a path to money and fame. Many states banned prizefighting for its cruelty. Others tried to manage the violence of the sport by limiting rounds to three minutes, dividing boxers into classes by weight, and requiring boxers to wear protective gloves.

The boxer who provoked the greatest reaction was Jack Johnson. Johnson was an African American athlete from Texas. In 1903 he became the heavyweight champion of African American boxers after beating "Denver" Ed Martin in the ring. Johnson wanted to fight the white heavyweight boxers, but at that time, whites and African Americans rarely boxed together. Top-ranking boxer Jim Jeffries, who was white, refused to challenge Johnson in a fight.

Johnson wanted to find other boxers who would fight him, so he decided to travel overseas. In 1908 he fought Tommy Burns, the world-champion boxer from Australia. Johnson trounced Burns and won a whopping thirty thousand dollars. Johnson was boxing's new world champion.

Back home, reporters called for a "great white hope" to regain the heavyweight championship from Johnson. Besides preferring a white world champ, many Americans disapproved of Johnson's personal life. The boxer flouted narrow-minded customs of the day by dating and marrying white women.

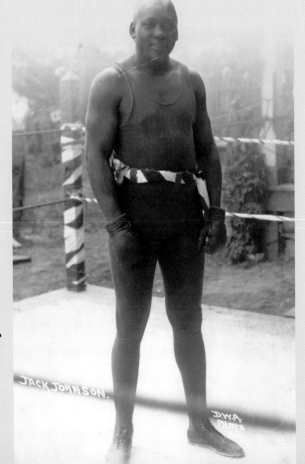

JACK JOHNSON stands in a boxing ring before a fight in the early 1900s.

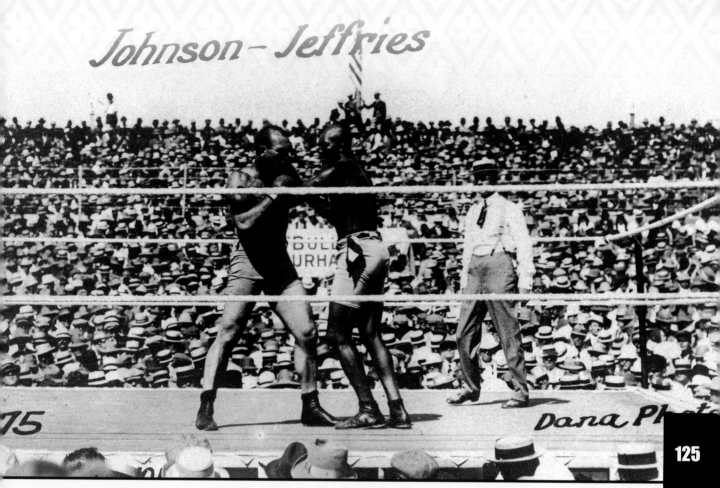

Johnson–Jeffries

JIM JEFFRIES *(LEFT)* AND JACK JOHNSON *(MIDDLE)* faced off in a ring built especially for the 1910 fight in Reno, Nevada.

Jeffries took the bait for the fight against Johnson. The fighter came out of retirement with the intention of beating the African American boxer who dared to date white women. But Johnson couldn't be defeated. Even though the white crowd harassed him, he beat Jeffries in the 1910 fight.

Johnson's win over Jeffries caused a huge sensation. Filmmakers wanted to make movies about the fight. Congress tried to ban films of the Johnson-Jeffries showdown, deeming it too controversial to show an African American athlete knocking down a white competitor—but a film about the fight did come out in 1910. The film, titled *The Jeffries-Johnson Fight,* featured footage captured by nine cameramen who had filmed the fight as it took place. It opened in northern states and overseas before a 1912 U.S. law banned transporting fight films interstate. But the film continued to appear at secret showings in African American neighborhoods.

■ THE OLYMPIC GAMES

Like boxing, the Olympic Games elicited a great deal of excitement among Americans of the early 1900s. In the 1900 Olympics in Paris, women gained the right to compete for the first time. Margaret Abbott of Chicago, Illinois, won a gold medal in golf.

The 1900 Olympics saw another first as well. Alvin Kraenzlein, a native of Milwaukee, Wisconsin, became the first Olympic athlete to win four gold medals in track and field. His novel open-scissors jumping technique earned him world records for hurdles and long jumps that have not been broken to this day.

In 1904 the United States hosted its first Olympics ever—in Saint Louis, Missouri. Only twelve countries participated in the games. Many refused to cope with weeks of travel by ship across the Atlantic Ocean. This left the field open for the United States to run away with the gold. American athletes grabbed top honors in twenty-one events. Two highlights of the 1904 games involved gymnast George Eyser and track-and-field star Ray Ewry. With a wooden leg, Eyser won six medals that year. Until the 2008 Olympics, Eyser was the only person with an

Olympic officials judge **TRACK STAR RAY EWRY** in the standing high jump in the 1904 Olympic Games. Ewry won gold medals in the standing high jump, standing long jump, and standing triple jump events.

The 1904 Olympics were part of **THE WORLD'S FAIR**, a huge celebration of world culture and international trade held in St. Louis, Missouri.

Lorz thought it good fun to go along with the ruse. He even took part in the awards ceremony. But soon it was revealed that he had caught a ride, and he was banned from athletics forever. Lorz regained favor in time to compete in and win the Boston Marathon of 1905. But his practical joke cast a shadow over the Olympics that remained until the close of games.

While not as dramatic as the Lorz scandal, another event caused a stir in the 1908 Olympics. The games that year took place in London, England. American athlete Ralph Rose had been chosen to carry the U.S. flag into London's Olympic stadium. But when he approached the British king's royal box, he refused to follow protocol and lower the flag as a sign of respect for the monarch. Rose claimed that the United States recognized no earthly king. Because of Rose's protest, British judges were tough on U.S. athletes competing in that year's games. All the same, Ewry managed to win thirteen of twenty-four track events, earning ten gold medals. His record still stood in 2009.

artificial leg to compete in the Olympics. Indiana-born Ewry had survived childhood polio and won three standing jump events in the 1904 Olympics.

While many people enjoyed the United States' 1904 Olympic successes, the competition was marred by a spectacular cheating scandal. New Yorker Fred Lorz became exhausted while running a marathon race, and he accepted a ride in an official's car at the 9-mile (14 km) mark. Then Lorz got out of the car near the finish line and jogged to the stadium to retrieve his clothes. Olympic fans and judges saw Lorz enter the stadium and mistakenly thought he had run the race. The judges declared him the winner.

■ RACING ON WHEELS

Bicycle racing was immensely popular throughout the early 1900s. Spectators from all walks of life thrilled to the speed and endurance required in bike racing. During outdoor bike races, fans gathered at velodromes—steeply banked oval tracks especially designed for bike riding. At the beginning of the twentieth century, most cities had such tracks. They allowed for smoother riding than muddy, potholed roads. Race organizers created carnival atmospheres around the velodromes. They played up the fanfare and excitement of bike races.

While bicycle racing remained popular throughout the 1900s, another sport on wheels soon began to take hold. That sport was auto racing. As factories began to deliver larger numbers of passenger cars, manufacturers decided that racing was a good way to advertise their product.

Henry Ford got in on the auto-racing craze. He hired Barney Oldfield—a former bicycle racer—to race his eighty-horsepower car called the *999*. Soon local auto clubs began to follow Ford's lead. They arranged races that attracted thousands of car enthusiasts. A new era in sports—and technology—had begun.

Henry Ford *(right)* stands next to his **FORD *999* RACE CAR** in 1904. Barney Oldfield sits at the wheel, ready for a race across a frozen lake in Michigan.

*M*arshall "Major" Taylor was an outstanding bicycle racer of the early 1900s. Born in Indianapolis, Indiana, in 1878, Taylor had had a love affair with bicycles since his first job with Hay & Willits—an Indianapolis bicycle shop. It was there he gained the nickname Major for wearing a military costume while performing bicycle tricks in the street to attract customers.

Taylor won his first race against professional cyclists when he was thirteen years old. He continued to beat pros throughout the Midwest. But because he was African American, prejudice often interfered with his ability to enter races, which were typically limited to white cyclists. Taylor moved to Worcester, Massachusetts, a more open-minded city. After training in his new home, Taylor topped the best racers in the United States.

By 1900 Taylor had won a world championship in Montreal, Canada, and set a new world record for the 1-mile (1.6 km) race—one minute, nineteen seconds. In 1901 he competed in his first European tour, outpacing the French world champion in Paris. The defeat so outraged the French track director that he paid Taylor's prize money in small coins that had to be hauled away in a wheelbarrow.

Although racist attitudes of the era kept some racing fans from accepting Taylor, he appealed to many people with his enormous talent and sharp intelligence. Most spectators went wild after his lightning-fast

MARSHALL "MAJOR" TAYLOR poses on his bicycle in a 1903 picture.

129

finishes and booed rivals who tried to force him off the track. White organizers included him in professional races because he drew crowds, earning everyone more money.

Still, Taylor often competed in Europe and Australia to avoid the racism he encountered in the United States. He found that fans and other cyclists overseas cared more about talent than skin color.

As a national and international champion racer, Taylor became only the second African American to win world-class titles, behind boxer George Dixon. He bested top racers on three continents before retiring in 1910.

Visitors enter THE ALASKA-YUKON-PACIFIC EXPOSITION
in Seattle in 1909. The huge fair promoted opportunities for trade with
Japan and for exploration and investment in the U.S. territory of Alaska.

Epilogue
STARS AND STRIPES
FOREVER

The first decade of the 1900s came to a close with much the same enthusiasm as it had begun. The United States remained in the limelight as a major world power. American presence in Latin America and the Pacific continued to be strong, even though the Taft administration intervened less than Roosevelt in the business of other nations.

Social reformers vowed to continue opposing unequal, unfair, and dangerous conditions at work, schools, and in neighborhoods. Employee and women's organizations coordinated to increase membership. They organized successful marches, strikes, and walkouts that won public support throughout the nation and became a strong tool for change.

At the same time, racial and ethnic prejudice faced many people in American society. For example, hundreds of immigrants who had viewed the United States as a beacon of hope and progress began to lose faith. Faced with poverty and bigotry, some gave up and went home.

A HOPEFUL FUTURE

Still, most Americans believed that the decade had spurred progress toward achieving a better world. They believed in the American dream of success through hard work and creativity, and they were filled with hope for themselves and their families. Educational opportunities reached an all-time high, and daily life improved with each new invention. For the first time, government spoke out to preserve the nation's natural resources. Going into the 1910s, Americans felt optimistic about their future.

1900

- William McKinley defeats William Jennings Bryan a second time to become U.S. president.
- Female factory workers organize the group that later becomes the International Ladies' Garment Workers Union.
- Bubonic plague hits Chinatown in San Francisco, California.
- Scott Joplin's "Maple Leaf Rag" first appears in print.
- L. Frank Baum publishes *The Wonderful Wizard of Oz*.

1901

- Anarchist Leon Czolgosz shoots and kills President McKinley.
- Vice President Theodore Roosevelt, aged forty-two, becomes the United States' youngest president.
- The United States occupies Cuba.
- President Roosevelt invites African American leader Booker T. Washington to dinner at the White House, creating friction with some racist government officials.
- Annie Edson Taylor becomes the first person to survive a descent over Niagara Falls in a barrel.

1902

- U.S. occupation of Cuba ends, and Cuba becomes an independent republic.
- Ida Tarbell begins publishing her series of articles the "History of the Standard Oil Company" in McClure's Magazine.
- Rose and Morris Michtom begin selling teddy bears, inspired by President Roosevelt.
- Stanford University and the University of Michigan teams play the first New Year's Day Rose Bowl game.

1903

- Orville and Wilbur Wright complete their famous airplane flight, traveling 852 feet (259 m) in fifty-nine seconds at Kitty Hawk, North Carolina.
- African American Maggie Walker opens the Saint Luke Penny Savings Bank in Richmond, Virginia, becoming the first woman bank president in the United States.
- Boston beats Pittsburgh in the first World Series.
- Mary "Mother" Jones takes a group of child laborers on a march from the Liberty Bell in Philadelphia, Pennsylvania, to President Roosevelt's summer home on Long Island, New York, to call for child labor laws.

1904

- President Roosevelt defeats Alton Parker by the largest majority in U.S. history for his first and only elected term as president.
- The United States begins construction on the Panama Canal.
- Russia and Japan go to war.

1904
- The U.S. Supreme Court breaks up John Pierpont Morgan's Northern Securities Company after determining that it violates the Sherman Anti-Trust Act.

1905
- W. E. B. DuBois and other noted African Americans form the Niagara Movement to promote African American rights.
- At a meeting in Chicago, Illinois, labor leaders establish the Industrial Workers of the World (IWW).
- President Roosevelt assigns administration of the federal forest reserves to the United States Forest Service under the Transfer Act.
- Nineteen high school and college athletes die due to football injuries, prompting the formation of the National Collegiate Athletic Association to oversee college sports.

1906
- President Roosevelt wins the Nobel Peace Prize for his role in negotiating the treaty that ends the Russo-Japanese War.
- The San Francisco earthquake kills approximately twenty-five hundred people and devastates the city.
- Upton Sinclair publishes his novel *The Jungle*, which exposes unsanitary conditions in Chicago stockyards.
- Congress passes the Pure Food and Drug Act to safeguard the foods and medical drugs that Americans rely on.

1907
- Leo Baekeland's invention of Bakelite produces the first synthetic plastic.
- Mutt and Jeff becomes the first well-known daily comic strip.
- The U.S. Army buys two hydrogen balloons to explore the possibilities of floating aircraft.
- Buck's Stove and Range Company arranges for a court order to prevent the American Federation of Labor (AFL) from writing about the company's antiunion policies in the AFL publication the *American Federationist*.

1908
- William Howard Taft is elected the twenty-seventh president of the United States.
- Henry Ford introduces the Model T automobile.
- Sears, Roebuck and Co. debuts its Modern Homes program, allowing customers to order build-your-own houses through the mail.

1909
- Explorer Robert Peary, his aide Matthew Henson, and four Inuit men make a historic journey to the North Pole.
- The New York Women's Trade Union League calls a textile workers' strike to demand better working conditions.
- Hazel Hotchkiss Wightman earns the first of her four wins in the U.S. Women's Championship tennis games.

SOURCE NOTES

7   Harold Evans, *The American Century* (New York: Alfred Knopf, 2000), 55.

7   William King, "Business Outlook for 1900," *New York Times,* January 1, 1900, AFR10.

12   *New York Times,* "Mr. Roosevelt Is Now the President," September 15, 1901.

13   Walter Lord, *The Good Years: From 1900 to the First World War* (New York: Harper & Brothers, 1960), 64–65.

14   BBC, "Building the Canal: New World Success," *BBC News,* December 8, 1999, http://news.bbc.co.uk/2/hi/americas/553149.stm (January 5, 2009).

14   Myra Immell, ed., *The 1900s* (San Diego: Greenhaven Press, 2000), 24.

17   Gunnar Knudsen, "The Nobel Peace Prize 1906: Presentation Speech," *Nobel Foundation,* n.d., http://nobelprize.org/nobel _prizes/peace/laureates/1906/press.html (January 5, 2009).

18   Immell, 24.

18   Lisa Grunwald and Stephen J. Adler, *Letters of the Century, 1900–1999* (New York: Dial Press, 1999), 64.

19   Robert Peary, quoted in Henry Collins Walsh, "The Pole at Last: Commander Peary Describes His Crowning Achievement in Arctic Travel and Exploration," *New York Times,* October 1, 1910, http://query.nytimes.com/mem/archive-free/pdf?res=9A02E0D81239E433A25752C0A9669D946196D6CF (January 5, 2009).

24   *New York Times,* "Obituary: John Muir, Aged Naturist, Dead," December 25, 1914.

24   Sierra Club, "John Muir: A Brief Biography," *Sierra Club,* n.d., http://www.sierraclub.org/john_muir_exhibit (January 5, 2009).

26   Theodore Roosevelt, report to Congress, January 22, 1909, quoted in James D. Richardson, ed., *A Compilation of the Messages and Papers of the Presidents 1789–1897,* vol. 11 (Washington, DC: Government Printing Office, 1920), 1,417.

26   Roosevelt, quoted in Richardson, 1, 417.

29   Immell, 153.

31   Ibid., 240.

35   *Time,* "One Hundred Great Things," December 7, 1998, http://www.time.com/time/magazine/article/0,9171,989802,00.html (January 5, 2009).

38   Henry Raymont, "Freud-Jung Letters to Appear." *New York Times,* July 15, 1970.

39   NPR, "The Coffee Break," *NPR.org,* December 2, 2002, http://www.npr.org/programs/morning/features/patc/coffeebreak/index.html (January 5, 2009).

40   *Law & Order Magazine,* "Fuzz on Wheels—Colorful Cops Cut Crime," August 1968, in Harley Leete, ed., *The Best of Bicycling* (New York: Trident Press), 339.

41   Editors of Time-Life Books, *Dawn of the Century, 1900–1910* (Alexandria, VA: 1998), 166.

41   Catherine Gourley, *Wheels of Time: A Biography of Henry Ford* (Brookfield, CT: Millbrook Press, 1997), 27.

41   Gourley, 27.

45   Loretta Britten, ed., *Century of Flight* (Richmond: Time-Life Books, 1999), 35.

49   Lord, 69.

51   Editors of Time-Life Books, 31.

52   Martin Sheffer, *In Search of Democratic America: The Writings of Randolph S. Bourne* (Lanham, MD: Lexington Books, 2002), 156.

54   Joseph Gardner, *Labor on the March* (New York: Harper & Row, 1969), 80–81.

58   Penny Colman, *Mother Jones and the March of the Mill Children* (Brookfield, CT: Millbrook Press, 1994), 24.

58   Colman, 24.

59   Immell, 240.

64   National Museum of the American Indian, "School Bells and Haircuts," *Nmai.si.edu,* n.d., http://www.nmai.si.edu/exhibitions/who_stole_the_teepee/school/index.htm (January 5, 2009).

66   Sonja Keohane, "The Reservation Boarding School System in the United States, 1870–1928," *Twofrog.com,* June 3, 2008, http://www.twofrog.com/rezsch.html (January 5, 2009).

69   Mary McLeod Bethune, quoted in Val J. Halamandaris, "Mary McLeod Bethune," *Profiles in Caring,* n.d., http://www.nahc.org/NAHC/Val/Columns/SC10-6.html (January 5, 2009).

70 Booker T. Washington, quoted in PBS Online / WGBH, "People & Events: Booker T. Washington," *PBS*, 1999, http://www.pbs.org/wgbh/amex/1900peopleevents/pande3.html (January 5, 2009).

71 David T. Gilbert, "Niagara Movement at Harpers Ferry Centennial Commemoration," *National Park Service*, August 11, 2006, http://www.nps.gov/archive/hafe/niagara/history.htm (January 5, 2009).

72 Allen, Frederick Lewis, *The Big Change: America Transforms Itself, 1900–1950* (New York: HarperCollins, 1952), in Immell, 38.

76 Eleanor Flexnor, *Century of Struggle: The Woman's Rights Movement in the United States* (Cambridge, MA: Belknap Press, 1975), 249.

85 George Bobinski, *Carnegie Libraries: Their History and Impact on American Public Library Development* (Chicago: American Library Association, 1969), 47.

85 Chris Potter, "You Had to Ask," *Pittsburgh City Paper*, 1999, http://andrewcarnegie2.tripod.com/hadtoask292000.html (January 5, 2009).

91 Wright, 20.

92 Virginia McAlester and Lee McAlester, *A Field Guide to American Houses* (New York: Knopf, 1984), 440.

92 Frank L. Wright, *Frank Lloyd Wright: The Natural House* (New York: Horizon Press, 1954), 20.

93 Rosemary Thornton, "Sears Homes Old Catalog," *Old House Web*, n.d., http://www.oldhouseweb.com/architecture-and-design/sears-homes-old-catalog.shtml (January 5, 2009).

95 Life Publishing Company, "Charles Dana Gibson," *Herald Square Hotel*, 2008, http://www.heraldsquarehotel.com/CDGibson.htm (January 5, 2009).

100 "Out for a 1.10 Mile!" *Worcester Daily Telegram*, November 20, 1899, 1.

106 Thomas Edison, quoted in "American Treasures of the Library of Congress: Reason," *Library of Congress*, June 9, 2005, http://www.loc.gov/exhibits/treasures/trr018.html (January 6, 2009).

110 Benjamin Robert Tubb, "I'm Certainly Living a Rag-Time Life," *Public Domain Music*, n.d., http://www.pdmusic.org/1900s/00iclartl.txt (January 5, 2009).

111 Library of Congress, "History of Ragtime," *Performing Arts Encyclopedia*, n.d., http://memory.loc.gov/diglib/ihas/loc.natlib.ihas.200035811/default.html (January 5, 2009).

116 Sue Macy, *Winning Ways: A Photohistory of American Women in Sports* (New York: Henry Holt, 1996), 33.

117 Ibid.

118 *Chicago Daily Tribune*, "Twelve Thousand People Over-Tax Comiskey's Stands," April 23, 1900.

112 Marlene Targ Brill, *Winning Women in Basketball* (Hauppauge, NY: Barron's, 2000), 5.

SELECTED BIBLIOGRAPHY

Brill, Marlene Targ. *Let Women Vote!* Brookfield, CT: Millbrook Press, 1996. This title details the history of how American women got the right to vote.

———. *Winning Women in Baseball & Softball.* Hauppauge, NY: Barron's, 2000. Women involved in baseball and softball are the topic of this sports history overview.

Caplow, Louis. *The First Measured Century.* Washington, DC: AEI Press, 2001. Caplow points out major trends of the early 1900s.

Cassi-Scott, Jack. *Costume and Fashion in Color, 1760–1920.* New York: Macmillan Company, 1971. A review of fashions for men and women, this book provides an interesting look at clothing during the first two decades of the 1900s.

Chauner, David, and Michael Halstead. *The Tour de France Complete Book of Cycling.* New York: Villard Books, 1990. Chauner and Halstead discuss the interest in bicycling during the 1900s and highlight Marshall "Major" Taylor's place in bicycling history.

Cooper, John, Jr. *Pivotal Decades: The United States, 1900–1920.* New York: Norton, 1990. This book takes a critical look at politics in the early 1900s.

Crichton, Judy. *America 1900: The Turning Point.* New York: Henry Holt, 1998. This companion book to the PBS documentary *America 1900* explores the United States at the turn of the twentieth century.

Evans, Harold. *The American Century.* New York: Alfred Knopf, 2000. A look back at the twentieth century, this title offers some fascinating insights into various aspects of the 1900s.

Gardner, Louise. *Art Through the Ages.* New York: Harcourt, Brace & World, 1959. An art history classic, this book emphasizes art trends of the early 1900s.

Grunwald, Lisa, and Stephen J. Adler. *Letters of the Century: America 1900–1999.* New York: Dial Press, 1999. Grunwald and Adler offer a compilation of twentieth-century letters written by notable and ordinary people alike.

Immell, Myra, ed. *The 1900s.* San Diego: Greenhaven, 2000. This source provides a good overview of the 1900s.

Jennings, Peter. *The Century.* New York: Doubleday, 2001. Written by one the nation's most celebrated investigative reporters, this review of the twentieth century features unusual tidbits from the 1900s.

Lord, Walter. *The Good Years: From 1900 to the First World War.* New York: Harper & Brothers, 1960. Lord compares and contrasts the 1900s and 1910s in this selection.

McComb, David. *Sports: An Illustrated History.* New York: Oxford University Press, 1998. This title explores some athletic highlights of the early 1900s.

Morris, Edmund. *Theodore Rex.* New York: Random House, 2001. This book provides a complete look into the life of Theodore Roosevelt.

Time-Life editors. *People Who Shaped the Century.* Alexandria, VA: Time-Life Books, 1999. This overview highlights twentieth-century individuals who made a lasting impact on the world.

Wright, Frank L. *Frank Lloyd Wright: The Natural House.* New York: Horizon Press, 1954. Written by the architect himself, this book takes a look at the reasoning behind the Prairie style.

TO LEARN MORE

Books

Bartoletti, Susan Campbell. *Kids on Strike!* Boston: Houghton Mifflin, 1999. Bartoletti tells the stories of young labor leaders in the nineteenth and early twentieth centuries.

Benson, Michael. *William H. Taft.* Minneapolis: Twenty-First Century Books, 2005. Read about the life of William Howard Taft, supervisor of the Panama Canal project and president of the United States from 1909 to 1913.

Brill, Marlene Targ. *Marshall "Major" Taylor: World Champion Bicyclist, 1899–1901.* Minneapolis: Twenty-First Century Books, 2008. Learn more about bicyclist Marshall "Major" Taylor, who made a name for himself in the early 1900s by breaking through racial barriers to become a racing champion.

Callan, Jim. *America in the 1900s and 1910s.* New York: Facts on File, 2006. This book paints a detailed and engaging portrait of American life in the early part of the twentieth century.

DuTemple, Lesley A. *The Panama Canal.* Minneapolis: Twenty-First Century Books, 2003. DuTemple provides a fascinating discussion of the Panama Canal—a structure that took forty years to build. Maps, photographs, and primary-source quotations bring the canal's story to life.

Feinstein, Stephen. *The 1900s: From Teddy Roosevelt to Flying Machines.* Berkeley Heights, NJ: Enslow, 2006. This title affords an engaging overview of the United States as it transitioned into the twentieth century.

Gourley, Catherine. *Gibson Girls and Suffragists: Perceptions of Women from 1900 to 1918.* Minneapolis: Twenty-First Century Books, 2008. This award-winning selection examines society's views on women in the early twentieth century.

Krensky, Stephen. *Comic Book Century: The History of American Comic Books.* Minneapolis: Twenty-First Century Books, 2008. Krensky explores the history of comic books and reveals their impact on U.S. culture.

McPherson, Stephanie Sammartino. *Theodore Roosevelt.* Minneapolis: Twenty-First Century Books, 2005. This book provides interesting information about Theodore Roosevelt, the United States' twenty-sixth president.

McPherson, Stephanie Sammartino, and Joseph Sammartino Gardner. *Wilbur & Orville Wright: Taking Flight.* Minneapolis: Twenty-First Century Books, 2003. After years of research and countless failed designs, the Wright Brothers succeeded in going where no man had gone before.

Miller, Ernestine. *Making Her Mark: Firsts and Milestones in Women's Sports.* New York: McGraw-Hill, 2002. This review of women in athletics covers key events, records, and firsts in sixty different sports.

Skurzynski, Gloria. *Sweat and Blood: A History of U.S. Labor Unions.* Minneapolis: Twenty-First Century Books, 2009. Read all about the fascinating history of labor unions and learn how they shaped the United States.

Films

America 1900. DVD. Boston: WGBH, 1998. This four-part documentary from PBS explores the United States at the turn of the twentieth century.

Henry Ford: Tin Lizzy Tycoon. DVD. New York: A&E, 2006. Learn more about the life of Henry Ford, revolutionary 1900s inventor and businessperson.

Wright Brothers' Flying Machine. DVD. Boston: NOVA, 2003. See footage of Wilbur and Orville Wright's historic flights, and watch as a team of aviation experts aims to re-create the Wright brothers' flying machine.

Websites

American Cultural History: The Twentieth Century
http://kclibrary.lonestar.edu/decades.html
This site from the Lone Star College-Kingwood College Library in Texas provides useful overviews of each decade of U.S. cultural history in the twentieth century.

American Memory Timeline
http://memory.loc.gov/learn/features/timeline/index.html
This Library of Congress page links to primary sources on a variety of U.S. history topics. It covers the years 1763 to 1968 and includes materials such as firsthand recollections of how cars changed the United States and immigrants' stories of life in their new homeland.

America's Story
http://www.americaslibrary.gov/cgi-bin/page.cgi
This website from the Library of Congress includes biographies of famous Americans, original historic documents, and discussions of different times in U.S. history.

1900–1909: The Turn of a Century
http://library.thinkquest.org/J0111064/00home.html
Thinkquest offers an overview of American fashion, events, entertainment, and more from the early 1900s.

SELECTED 1900s CLASSICS

Books

Baum, L. Frank. *The Wonderful Wizard of Oz.* New York: Signet Classics, 2006. The enchanted journey of Dorothy and her dog, Toto, has captured readers' imaginations since Baum first published *The Wonderful Wizard of Oz* in 1900.

London, Jack. *Call of the Wild.* New York: Aladdin Paperbacks, 2003. London's 1903 tale tells of a kidnapped pet dog who must learn to survive in the harsh world of the Yukon territory.

Tarbell, Ida M. *The History of the Standard Oil Company.* Mineola, NY: Dover Publications, 2003. Tarbell's 1902–1904 article series exposing the business practices of Standard Oil is presented in book format in this fascinating volume.

Films

The Gay Shoe Clerk, 1904
In this brief 1904 picture, a shoe clerk gets in trouble after he shares a kiss with a flirtatious female customer. Music by Scott Joplin accompanies the film. You can watch it on YouTube at http://www.youtube.com/watch?v=Q2X_BZpnWFc.

The Great Train Robbery, 1903
A silent Western lasting 11.2 minutes, *The Great Train Robbery* features two bandits who try to rob a train depot agent. You can watch it on YouTube at http://www.youtube.com/watch?v=Bc7wWOmEGGY.

Life of an American Fireman, 1903
This six-minute film depicts firefighters arriving by horse and buggy to save a helpless family from a dangerous blaze. You can watch it on YouTube at http://www.youtube.com/watch?v=p4C0gJ7BnLc.

1900s ACTIVITY

Identify six to ten things in everyday life that relate to the early 1900s. (To start you thinking, consider family antiques or collections, your house or buildings in your neighborhood, movies, books, or songs you may have heard of, and places you've visited.) Use photographs, mementos, and words to create a paper or electronic scrapbook of your 1900s connections.

INDEX

141

ABOUT THE AUTHOR

Marlene Targ Brill has written many books for young adults, including *Tourette Syndrome*, *Marshall "Major" Taylor: World Champion Bicyclist, 1899–1901*, and several books in The Decades of Twentieth-Century America series.

PHOTO ACKNOWLEDGMENTS